GLAMORGAN

THE GLORY YEARS 1993-2002

Top: Four of Glamorgan`s England men – Matthew Maynard, Steve Watkin, Robert Croft and Hugh Morris. *Bottom:* Two of the other key players in recent years – Adrian Dale (left) and Steve James (right), who also won England caps, after making the highest individual score in the club's history, scoring 309* against Sussex at Colwyn Bay in 2000.

GLAMORGAN

THE GLORY YEARS 1993-2002

Andrew Hignell

TEMPUS

*This book is dedicated to the memory of Byron Denning,
Glamorgan's official scorer from 1983 to 2001.*

First published 2003

PUBLISHED IN THE UNITED KINGDOM BY:
Tempus Publishing Ltd
The Mill, Brimscombe Port
Stroud, Gloucestershire GL5 2QG

PUBLISHED IN THE UNITED STATES OF AMERICA BY:
Tempus Publishing Inc.
2 Cumberland Street
Charleston, SC 29401

British Library Cataloguing in Publication Data.
A catalogue record for this book is available from the British Library.

ISBN 0 7524 2747 4

Typesetting and origination by Tempus Publishing.
Printed in Great Britain by Midway Colour Print, Wiltshire

Contents

Acknowledgements

This book could not have been written had it not been for the success of the Glamorgan players over the past decade or so, and their full co-operation in providing memories and reminiscences. In particular, I'm very grateful to Steve James, Steve Watkin, John Derrick, Michael Kasprowicz and Don Shepherd for providing more detailed reviews of events from the past and present, and also to Mike Fatkin, the club's chief executive, for travelling down memory lane to the time in the 1980s when he joined the club. Several other people who play an important role behind the scenes have also helped, including Caryl Watkin, Tony Ball, David Irving, Mark Frost, Roger Skyrme, Gordon Lewis, and last, but by no means least, the late Byron Denning and his wife Olwen.

Most of the splendid photographs which adorn this book come from the camera of Huw John, the club's honorary photographer, and as always, I'm grateful for his support. My thanks as well to the following for their photographic assistance – Alan Cozzi, Morton Davies, Peter Frost, Jen Little, Empics, Huw Evans, Stuart Franklin, Nigel French, George Herringshaw, Steve Kloppe, Paul McGregor, Graham Morris, David Munden, Andrew Orchard, Dave Pinegar, Bill Smith, Nick Treharne and Iolo Williams.

Amongst the other people and organisations I would like to offer thanks to are BBC Wales, *The Western Mail, The South Wales Echo, The South Wales Evening Post, The Wales on Sunday, The South Wales Argus*, Central Press Photos, Associated Sports Photography, the cartoonist 'Gren', Edward Bevan, John Billot, Phil Blanche, Peter Davies, Howard Evans, Bob Harragan, Trevor Jones, Rob Owen, Richard Thomas, Simon Thomas and Paul Tully as well as Brains, the club's current sponsor. Their association with Glamorgan CCC stretches back into the 1890s when Joseph Brain, and his brother William, were captain and wicketkeeper respectively of the Glamorgan Minor County side. Without their sterling efforts the county club might have folded before the First World War, never to experience these Glory Years.

Finally, a big thank you to James Howarth, Kate Wiseman, Ruth Potter and Becky Gadd of Tempus Publishing for their support and advice, as well as my wife Debra, as our dining room table disappeared again under a mound of photographs and paper!

Andrew Hignell
Wells, Somerset
April 2003

Foreword

by Don Shepherd (Glamorgan 1950-1972)

This book has been specifically compiled to commemorate and enlarge upon the successes of Glamorgan County Cricket Club since the 1990s. Particular attention is given to the period 1993-2002, possibly the most illustrious decade in the club's history. Indeed, the record books suggest that only the 1960s can offer any sort of challenge to that claim.

1993 was indeed a remarkable summer – third position in the Britannic Assurance County Championship, semi-finalists in the NatWest Trophy and proud winners of the AXA Equity & Law League – Glamorgan's first trophy since the Championship of 1969. The contest in mid-September on a balmy Sunday when nearest rivals Kent were beaten at Canterbury will live long in the memory. Certainly, this was one of the most memorable and emotional days for the many thousands of Welsh supporters present – myself included. Hugh Morris

Don Shepherd.

and his victorious team, which included the great Sir Vivian Richards, had a just claim to be the equal of any in the club's history.

Apart from losing the NatWest semi-final against Warwickshire in 1996, little of note was achieved until 1997, when somewhat unexpectedly, Glamorgan won their third Championship under the imaginative captaincy of Matthew Maynard; twenty-seven years after Tony Lewis' team triumphed in 1969 and all but half a century after Wilfred Wooller's 1948 team famously won Glamorgan's first Championship, an event which deserves a special place in Welsh sporting history and one which firmly and finally established the County as a major force in the game.

Maynard was still in charge as the County battled their way to the Benson & Hedges Final in 2000. There were high hopes that they would achieve what Alan Jones' team had failed to do in the 1977 Gillette Final against Middlesex – win a title at English cricket's HQ. Despite the skipper's wonderful century, it was not to be and Gloucestershire – the acknowledged masters of one-day tactics – were too good. Glamorgan did not leave with the title, but nothing could detract from the special Welsh atmosphere in St John's Wood on that very special day.

Season 2001 was notable for the consistency of Glamorgan's cricket in Division Two of the Norwich Union League. Under new captain Steve James, the team had a plan which they adhered to and 11 wins was proof of its effectiveness – enough too for the Glamorgan Dragons to resist the challenge of the Durham Dynamos and Worcestershire Royals and earn promotion – a terrific performance from James and his team.

At the start of 2002, the burning question was would Glamorgan be able to maintain their new status amongst the quality teams in Division One of the Norwich Union League? The answer was that they certainly could and did, and they also exceeded all expectations by becoming Champions, winning all of their away games to improve on their achievements in 2001 when they had been unbeaten at home.

Their successful tactics that had been so effective in their promotion drive in 2001 were followed once more, and again they proved to be successful. Glamorgan's wonderful fielding qualities deserve special mention, and often proved to be the vital difference between themselves and their opponents, as many games went down to the wire in close finishes. Indeed, the title clincher – on another sunny Sunday at Canterbury – was a fine advert for the character and strengths of the whole Glamorgan squad, and winning the Norwich Union League was a fantastic climax to the decade of Glamorgan Cricket which this book covers.

The 1960s were possibly the only other era in the club's history that comes within range of matching the achievements of the past ten seasons, and by pointing out some of the highlights from the 1960s, my intention is to provide points of interest and not,

The victorious Glamorgan team gather on the balcony of the pavilion at Bournemouth after their victory over Hampshire which secured the 1948 Championship title.

Top: The Glamorgan team of 1969. From left to right, back row: Eifion Jones, Bryan Davis, Malcolm Nash, Lawrence Williams, Roger Davis, Majid Khan. Front row: Tony Cordle, Peter Walker, Tony Lewis, Don Shepherd, Alan Jones. *Bottom:* Tony Lewis and his team gather for a special dinner in Cardiff City Hall after Glamorgan had become County Champions in 1969.

The crowd run onto St Helen's after Glamorgan's famous victory over the South Africans in 1951.

in any way, to deflect any credit from the magnificent achievements of our contemporary Glamorgan cricketers.

However, it is as well to consider how much the game has evolved since that period, especially the development of skills required to succeed in the intense atmosphere of the limited-over contests. Athletic fielding, controlled bowling and inventive batting are all now expected as the norm. The degree of planning is also far more prominent than in those earlier days when, upon reflection, it seems to me that any shortened version of the game was just that and approached with less thought than is now vital to succeed.

Although the Gillette Cup began in 1963 and the John Player League in 1969, the emphasis then was entirely based on the County Championship, augmented by highly anticipated fixtures against touring teams, and a chance for us in Wales to pit our wits and skills against some of the finest Test players in world cricket.

The 1960 season marked the conclusion of Wilf Wooller's long and influential reign. He had been the cornerstone of the club since the end of the Second World War, and had led the side to their famous Championship victory in 1948 – a year which for me was spent on the groundstaff at Lord's learning my trade as a bowler and a professional cricketer.

Wilf's last year as captain saw the team finish in eleventh position in the county table. Ossie Wheatley, who had joined the club from Warwickshire, then took over the captaincy, and there were a couple of indifferent seasons until 1963, when Glamorgan shot up the table to occupy second place. The following year we defeated the Australians at Swansea, and in 1965 Glamorgan finished in third place in the Championship.

Ossie handed over the reins to Tony Lewis in 1968, and under Tony's skilful leadership, the club enjoyed a mini golden era – third place in 1968, plus another victory over Australia, County Champions in 1969 and, just for good measure, runners-up to Kent in 1970, by virtue of having fewer bonus points.

So despite the ups and downs that have always seemed to be part and parcel of the affairs of Glamorgan County Cricket Club, the 1960s saw the club finish in the top three of the county table on four occasions, but there was no one-day success whatsoever.

During those years, the club's proud traditions and record against touring teams were enhanced by defeating the Pakistanis at Cardiff Arms Park in 1962 and then, famously, the Australians at St Helen's ground, Swansea in their successive tours of 1964 and 1968. We also just missed out on defeating the South Africans in 1965 after making them follow-on, and when the game finished, we were two wickets away from another touring scalp, having beaten them at Swansea in 1951.

For many years, Glamorgan had plum fixtures against touring teams over the Whitsun holiday in Cardiff and through the August bank holiday weekend at Swansea –

Don Shepherd (right) and Barry Jarman are surrounded by a happy crowd of Glamorgan supporters after the county's victory over the Australian tourists at Swansea in 1968.

A Western Mail cartoon from the 1920s.

much to the delight of the County's treasurer, who could depend on substantial gate money, and to us as players.

For many in the Glamorgan side, these games against the touring teams provided the only chance for us to test our skills against international crick-eters, and these games were treated with the greatest of respect by ourselves and the tourists alike. Often these encounters were viewed by the national press as extra Test matches.

It had been my pleasure to first play against a touring team in May 1950 – my first year on the Glamorgan staff – when the great West Indian team visited Cardiff Arms Park, with a side containing Frank Worrell, Everton Weekes, Clyde Walcott, 'Sonny' Ramadhin and Alf Valentine. It was a real thrill for me then, as a young fast-bowler, to play against the three Ws, and those two fine spinners, immortalised in that famous calypso, Ramadhin and Valentine.

That game, in Cardiff in 1950, ended in an innings victory for the tourists, but the following year Glamorgan become the only County side to defeat the touring South Africans, and it was on 6 August 1951 that I really became aware of how much victory, especially one over a Test team, meant to Glamorgan's many, many supporters. Much has been written about that dramatic match, suffice to say that on the second afternoon, a South African victory looked more likely than a Welsh one, as the visitors, chasing 148 for victory, took tea at 54 without loss. What happened in the following three-quarters of an hour is part of the club's folklore, as all ten wickets fell for just 29 runs against those two brilliant off-spinners Len Muncer and Jim McConnon, who shrewdly exploited a drying pitch and engineered a fine triumph amidst great excitement.

Returning to the 1960s, our back-to-back wins over the Australians at Swansea were very different in their execution. To an extent, our win in 1964 by 36 runs rescued what had been a fairly poor season. On a pitch responding to spin, Jim Pressdee and myself shared the bulk of the wickets, but tribute must be paid firstly to Glamorgan's batsmen for providing enough runs from which to set a target, and secondly, the youthful Glamorgan side who were simply outstanding in the field, and maintained the fine traditions of fielding that Wilf Wooller and his side of 1948 had established.

As it happened, the National Eisteddfod of 1964 was also being staged in Swansea at the same time as our magnificent game against the Australians, and that great broad-caster – the late Alun Williams – who was working there for the BBC said that as more and more Australian wickets fell at St Helen's, huge crowds were gathered around the little black and white televisions situated around the 'Maes'. Marvellous!

There was a fine atmosphere again four years later, when the 1968 Australians visited Swansea, and once again our batsman supplied plenty of runs, whilst the wickets were shared between seam and spin. In the absence of Tony Lewis, who was struck down with a throat infection, I deputised as leader, and despite Tony's absence, the boys rose to the occasion again, especially in the field. Our catching was razor sharp as we asked the Aussies to chase 365 on the final day. Despite a fine hundred from Paul Sheahan, we remained on top, and once again the post-match victory celebrations were typically Welsh, enjoyed by ourselves and the Australians, who were extremely sporting in defeat.

The County Championship success of 1969 brought that era to its close. There then began an era much different from the previous ten years, and a time when overseas players were first making their mark in the county game. In Pakistani Majid Khan and West Indian Bryan Davis, the Glamorgan side of 1969 had two fine batsmen, both of whom played many valuable innings and helped Tony Lewis clinch the club's first silverware since the days of Wooller and Clay back in 1948.

Glamorgan County Cricket Club now commences its journey into the twenty-first century under circumstances very different from those summers in the sixties, as well

The Glamorgan team walking off the Arms Park after beating Sussex to win their inaugural County Championship match in 1921.

Tony Cordle and other members of the Glamorgan side gather on the balcony of the Sophia Gardens pavilion after beating Worcestershire to become the County Champions of 1969.

as the days back in the 1920s when the club was initially accepted into the County Championship. These were the years when the County side was composed of happy-go-lucky amateurs, a small group of well-travelled professionals and a small measure of home-grown talent, all held together by the wafer-thin finances and heady dreams of captains such as Norman Riches, Johnnie Clay and latterly Maurice Turnbull, all of whom remained determinedly optimistic, despite many reverses, year after year.

The county game and the fortunes of Glamorgan CCC have come a long way since May 1921 when Glamorgan won their inaugural County Championship match, against Sussex at the Arms Park. This is the case both off the field as well as on it – no longer does the club rent a small office in Cardiff city centre, or hire the use of various grounds in South Wales for their home fixtures. There now exists a top-class headquarters at Sophia Gardens with brilliant practice facilities, back-up staff able to cater for any eventuality and an academy structure – so essential for survival in an increasingly finance-orientated game that favours the wealthy Counties. This structure supplies home-produced, and trained, young and talented cricketers who are already making their presence felt, thanks to the hard work of many fine coaches, including Steve Watkin, one of the bowling stalwarts of these glory years.

The future of the club appears to be in safe hands and if the next ten years proves to be as interesting as the last, then we will enjoy much more good Glamorgan cricket.

1

Laying the Foundations
by Mike Fatkin

I can still recall vividly the first day I spent working for Glamorgan. It was 21 April 1986 and I was a fresh-faced, long-haired ex-student with a degree in media and communication studies (and a Masters in naivety!), who'd not worn a tie in years, and who'd somehow persuaded the then secretary Philip Carling to let me have a crack at cricket administration on a trial basis.

At the time I considered it a triumph for my negotiating skills. I'd written to all of the counties after graduating and although I was rather optimistically expecting to go straight into a senior manager's job at a Test Match ground, the offers hadn't exactly come flooding in, though Glamorgan had invited me to make the 12-hour round trip by train to 'pop in for a chat'. Philip explained to me that it didn't quite work like that and having entered the building with thoughts of a £30,000 salary, with pension and car, I eventually settled for his suggestion that it would be positively life-changing for me to relocate from Yorkshire and work for Glamorgan for next to nothing for six months.

I can remember leaving Sophia Gardens on a high. By the time I'd got home, reality had kicked in. Had I been conned? I knew little about Glamorgan, about county cricket, indeed about work in general, this being my first – and so far only! – 'proper job'. Okay, so I enjoyed cricket, but here I was accepting a bit of pocket money and some digs and a few well-intentioned words of encouragement about how there might be a bit of a career in there for me if I put my head down. It probably wasn't what I'd had in mind, although with the benefit of hindsight it certainly proved an important decision for me, hopefully for the club as well. They've certainly had their two-penny half-penny's worth from me over the years!

Most of the first few months were a bit of a blur. Among the first people I met were Matthew Maynard, Hugh Morris, Ian Smith and Philip North, all still good friends, and all the same sort of age as me. I could identify with them because of that. I can remember being a bit star-struck when Philip Carling introduced me to Greg Thomas, only a few days back from the England tour of the West Indies. I also recall being in Philip's office when Somerset came to town and where Ian Botham – fresh from tabloid stories about him having confessed to smoking cannabis – was sheltering from the hacks. Ian Botham! Trying to strike up a conversation with him perhaps wasn't exactly the most sensible thing I've attempted to do. After all, we had so much in common: him a sporting icon and legend and me, well, you get the picture. I can't remember what the nature of the conversation was, but he must have (rightly!) thought I was a complete prat.

Those early years were great fun. There was little in the way of responsibility, and my jobs ranged from collating marketing contacts, to inputting membership data, to

A smiling Mike Fatkin (right) with Hugh Davies (Cricket Chairman) and Duncan
Fletcher (coach) and the Championship trophy in 1997.

running errands, all conducted in the palatial surroundings of what we now affection-
ately term 'the old offices'. In October 1985, Glamorgan's administrative HQ was in the
centre of Cardiff – they'd only moved to Sophia Gardens five months before I came
blundering in and I've since learned just how hard people had to work to make even
that step forward. As a club, we had little. No ground, a playing record that was on the
very modest side of ordinary, and a sporadic England representation. But humble
though we were, we had ambition as an organisation and we also had a very solid
commercial base and some good people exploiting it. What we lacked was a catalyst.

With an ordinary team, the fact that we had no control over our ground also made
it difficult to attract players. Without an indoor facility in Cardiff (the nearest was in
Neath) and with poor outdoor practice facilities (and what we did have, we generally
ended up having to argue over), our image around the county circuit was of a cricketing backwater; pleasant enough, but unsuccessful and somewhat gypsy-like, though
our reputation as 'doers' was growing. By the mid-1990s – thanks in part to fantastic
support from Anderson Consulting, and Paul Russell in particular, in helping to
transform our profile – Glamorgan were seen as innovators. Back in the late 1980s,
though, I recall travelling regularly with Tony Dilloway (my sparring partner for what
would prove to be fifteen years) to such exotic, far-flung outposts as Aberystwyth,
Ebbw Vale, Merthyr, Llanelli and Colwyn Bay, first to negotiate with them for the
staging of Glamorgan matches, and then to set everything up – stands, medical
facilities, marquees, pitches, scoreboards, stewards, you name it. We felt like circus
promoters.

We didn't own Sophia Gardens. We were restricted in terms of how much cricket we
could play there, and with added restrictions at Swansea because of the rugby season

we were inevitably reliant on other outgrounds as a means of generating income, especially as our membership was low. Until the decision was taken in the mid-1990s that we had to acquire a base for our headquarters, we had little option but to continue with the policy. In 1988 we managed to play sixteen Sunday League games on sixteen different grounds! But they were happy days even if, on the face of it, Glamorgan continued to underachieve, rarely threatening the big boys. The cricket was cosy, relatively unpressured; staging internationals was something other people did, and running our own ground wasn't a responsibility we had to worry about.

So what were the catalysts that led to Glamorgan not only competing through the 1990s but actually winning titles? There was no single thing, more a combination of factors that came together.

There is a photograph in the old offices at Sophia Gardens of a Glamorgan Colts XI side, taken at Llandarcy in around 1987, when the Colts played in the South Wales Cricket Association. In that photo, alongside Jim Pressdee and Alan Jones, who ran the side, were the likes of Philip North and Michael Cann. More to the point, the picture also shows a series of fresh faces belonging to Steve James, Tony Cottey, Steve Watkin and Adrian Dale. A season or two later, and along came Robert Croft and David Hemp. Maybe it was luck, who knows, but the coaching programme the club instigated in the late 1980s delivered a batch of high-quality youngsters and when they were set

The Glamorgan squad of 1985. From left to right, back row: Byron Denning (First XI scorer), Matthew Maynard, Ian Smith, Les McFarlane, Steve Malone, John Derrick, Steve Henderson, Mark Price, Hugh Morris, Martin Roberts, Gordon Lewis (Second XI scorer). Front row: Greg Thomas, Geoff Holmes, Alan Lewis Jones, John Steele, Phil Carling (chief executive), Rodney Ontong (captain), Alan Jones (coach), John Hopkins, Younis Ahmed, Terry Davies, Steve Barwick.

alongside the likes of Matthew Maynard, Hugh Morris and Steve Barwick it was evident that, with careful nurturing, quality leadership and a couple of astute signings, Glamorgan could compete.

At the same time, the club had to make one or two successful signings from other counties to augment the talented youngsters who were emerging. In the close season of 1986/87, the club successfully persuaded Alan Butcher to join Glamorgan. 'Butch' had been a highly productive opening batsman for Surrey and his recruitment was a key turning point. Unlike some of the signings the club had made in the late 1970s and early to mid-1980s, he was a quality performer, and his record and influence prove that.

That same winter, Terry Davies – the regular wicketkeeper – opted to remain in Australia and took the decision to retire from the game. He needed to be replaced and, again, the player who came in proved to be a very important addition. Colin Metson, who had only had limited opportunities at Middlesex because of the presence of Paul Downton, took up the opportunity of First XI cricket offered by Glamorgan. Alan and Colin, in differing ways, helped strengthen the side, their skills and experience complementing those of the established players like Maynard and Morris, as well as the emerging youngsters.

Tony Lewis' appointment as chairman in 1988 heralded another important shift. He'd been there and done it all at both county and international level, and was well-respected throughout the game. Having originally agreed to rejoin the Glamorgan committee as cricket chairman, he was subsequently elected as the club's chairman in succession to Gwyn Craven. Gwyn had done much to help Glamorgan grow and develop, but having someone like Tony Lewis at the helm was always going to alter the outside perception of Glamorgan for the better.

Tony recognised that his work commitments wouldn't allow him to concentrate 100 per cent on Glamorgan all of the time but, as with his successors, David Morgan and Gerard Elias, I have never felt that this was a significant handicap. So long as they are available for key meetings and on the end of a telephone or an e-mail, then their influence isn't diluted in any way. Tony's appointment coincided with the appointment of David Morgan as his deputy. They proved an excellent partnership, Tony working on cricket and coaching matters and David on the commercial elements of the business. Along with Gerard, I believe Glamorgan to have been very fortunate to have had such good people at the helm throughout the period. The club has also benefited from fantastic off-field staff – supportive, hard-working, ambitious and totally committed to the cause. No success can be achieved without that.

One of Tony's strongly held views was that the club had to concentrate more on developing its own players. He believed that Glamorgan, as the Welsh county, had a duty to develop as many Welsh cricketers as possible. It's a philosophy that still exists today. What does success from a Welsh cricket team truly mean if that team isn't comprised of a large percentage of home-grown cricketers? There had to be a greater concentration on growing our own, supplementing them with recruits from elsewhere only where a gap existed and where absolutely necessary.

'Recruits' meant looking hard at the recruitment of overseas players, not just England-qualified ones. My first few months in 1986 had been dominated by Javed Miandad's decision not to return to Glamorgan. Whatever his reasons, the club even-

The Glamorgan Colts squad of 1986 – Steve James and Steve Watkin are standing second and third from the left, whilst Adrian Dale is third from the left in the front row. Tony Cottey is sitting on the far right, with captain Jim Pressdee sitting in the middle of the front row, and coach Alan Jones on the far left of the back row.

tually used Ezra Moseley – who was also playing league cricket in Lancashire – and Denis Hickey, a young Australian over in the UK on a scholarship. One of Tony's first recommendations was that we should be aiming higher. For the 1987 season, the club had signed Ravi Shastri, who proved both effective and highly popular, and with the then skipper Hugh Morris keen on the idea of a quick bowler as the second overseas player, South African Corrie Van Zyl had also been recruited. That didn't work out, Corrie returning home midway through the 1988 season, but the signing of Ravi was a taste of things to come.

In January 1989, I can remember being told that Glamorgan were going to sign Viv Richards. Viv Richards? At Glamorgan? I thought it was a joke. Since leaving Somerset in 1986 in rather acrimonious circumstances, Viv had played league cricket in Lancashire the following year and toured the UK with the West Indies in 1988, but although available, no one else had shown any interest. Some said he was over the hill. Perhaps. But if that were the case, I'd hate to have seen him in a Glamorgan side at his prime. Unfortunately, a medical condition ruled him out of joining Ravi for the 1989 season, although he came over during the match against the Australians at Neath in July that year to confirm that yes, he would be here in 1990; no, he wasn't 'over the hill'; and no, he wasn't joining Glamorgan just to make up the numbers. He was a winner and he fully expected to be winning things with Glamorgan. That he was persuaded to come at all was a triumph for the club. It was also, arguably, the single most important foundation stone in the building process.

The medical condition he was suffering from was painful – I know as I've had it! – and there was no way that he could play in 1989. The club was satisfied with the explanations and relaxed enough to stick with Viv and wait for the 1990 season, but that didn't stop people from writing letters, many obscene and racist, several threatening. He said he would be back, and he was. A century on his debut would have given him a lot of pleasure. Funny how those who were quick to mock the club for signing someone they perceived to be over the hill very soon turned into Richards converts – something that was to be repeated, albeit on a smaller scale, when Glamorgan signed Waqar Younis in 1997. Whether or not the game should be going for overseas players or not, and we all have our views, Glamorgan's track record with them post 1986 has been excellent – good players and good characters all.

I'd only met Viv Richards once before, in May 1986, the same match in which I'd attempted to engage Ian Botham in meaningful conversation, and this too was something of an inauspicious first meeting. I'd been sent to the dressing room to chase up a couple of bats we'd asked to be signed. One month into the job and dressing room protocol wasn't something I was too well versed in, so I just marched in and asked,

Four more for Alan Butcher.

Hugh Morris (left) and Tony Lewis (right) at Swansea.

'Would you mind signing these as I need them now?', to which the classic response came, in a deep, booming, Antiguan drawl – and I quote verbatim – 'Don't know who you are, man, but why don't you take your ******* bats and **** off outta my territory?' Fair enough. My school career high of 55 against Trent College in 1982 hadn't exactly elevated me to the pantheon of greatness so I suppose he had a point. First there'd been the cheek of Botham not striking up a conversation with me and then an hour or two later Richards is politely asking me to leave his dressing room for no apparent reason. Didn't they know who I was? Erm, no, as it happens.

Tony Lewis had wanted Viv to swagger to the middle, chewing gum, to dominate the crease, to inspire the dressing room, to boom out support in the field. He gave us that, and more. He gave Glamorgan credibility. He instilled in those around him a will to win, a never-say-die attitude. He was a winner and he expected his team-mates to be as well. His dominating personality may not have been everyone's cup of tea but his influence was massive. Conversely, he was a pussycat off the field: always supportive, friendly, polite and helpful. In short, he was exactly what Glamorgan needed at that time. His seasons with the club in 1990, 1992 and 1993 (West Indies were touring again in 1991) helped shape the decade and every time I look at the picture on the wall in the office of a tearful Viv Richards with Hugh Morris, at Canterbury in 1993, having just seen Glamorgan to their first title in 24 years and their first ever in one-day cricket, I am reminded of just how potent Viv's influence must have been. He gave the club belief.

Hugh Morris had been awarded the Glamorgan captaincy in July 1986 when Rodney Ontong stood down. He probably had no option but to accept the offer but he was just twenty-two, the same age as me. I don't know what was going through his mind in those early months, but I know I would have found it a difficult enough job at *any* age, let alone at twenty-two and only just established in the side, a side – lest anyone needs reminding – that was rooted to the foot of the table and had been for years. He carried on as captain until midway through the 1989 season, when, like Rodney, he chose to relinquish the job, in Hugh's case because he felt it was affecting his form. Within two years he was playing for England. I believe Hugh also came back a better captain when he took over again in 1993 – and promptly led Glamorgan to that one-day title – but I felt that it came too soon for him in 1986. I don't know whether he sees it that way, but I've always thought it was thrust on him a bit unfairly.

Hugh's resignation at Bristol in July 1989 elevated Alan Butcher to the captaincy and his appointment was another important cog in the wheel as far as the development of Glamorgan in the 1990s was concerned. Quiet, unassuming and unselfish, but ruthless where necessary and astute as a captain, Alan's leadership over the next few years, and the way he worked with Tony Lewis in particular, was important to the evolution of the side and his contribution as captain from 1989 to 1992 is often understated. In addition to his qualities as a captain, he was also the one who identified Matthew Maynard's leadership potential, awarding him the vice-captaincy in 1992. I can recall him telling me that he believed Matthew should be encouraged as it was his view he could make an excellent captain in the future and thinking, 'Is this the same Matt that I've grown up with?' Oh ye of little faith. How right he was.

When I first saw Matthew Maynard play I was just captivated. How he only played four Tests for England heaven only knows. Along with Botham, David Gower, and lately Andrew Flintoff, he was one of only a few England-qualified players I'd try to drop everything for and go and watch bat. That his development has run in parallel with Glamorgan's development from 'also rans' into genuine contenders can't be down purely to coincidence. He's quality. And he grew in stature as the decade went on.

Viv Richards.

Ravi Shastri.

There were of course other factors leading up to that 1993 season, but Tony Lewis's appointment as chairman, Alan Butcher's elevation to the captaincy (and Hugh Morris's consequent development as both a player and an improved captain when he took the job back), the concentration on youth development and the batch of high-quality youngsters emerging in the late 1980s were arguably the most significant. I also felt that Alan Jones's experience in helping first Hugh, and then 'Butch', in bringing on the younger players was a key factor. Glamorgan through and through, Alan had nurtured the likes of James, Dale, Hemp, Croft and Watkin and was able to ensure that they remained disciplined and focused as they graduated to a higher level. That's an influence that has been continued with the likes of Duncan Fletcher and Jeff Hammond, but perhaps the closest parallel is with John Derrick, a player in the 1980s who knows exactly what it's like to be a young cricketer making your name at Glamorgan. His influence in 2002 was significant for the same reason as Alan Jones's fifteen years before him.

The players will relate their memories themselves, and rightly so, because they are the ones we all watch, they are the ones we all want to succeed, and they are the ones who deliver the prizes when they come. But it's a journey we've all been on with them: supporters, back room staff, committee. We've lived every moment with them. If I'm honest it was the triumph in 1993 that I enjoyed the most – not just being there, but being in the office on the Monday after we'd secured the title, seeing the press cuttings, taking all the phone calls. It was the relief as much as anything else, relief at laying to rest a 24-year-long bogey and realizing that we could win, of seeing all of the work over the previous years come to fruition.

I probably didn't expect another success as little as four years later, especially as it was 'the big one', the Championship. With Matthew in charge, a Matthew I'd seen grow up so much from the permed-haired, moustachioed cavalier of 1986, and Duncan

Viv Richards
batting for
Glamorgan.

Hugh Morris receives an award when leading Young England against Young Australia in 1983.

Alan Jones – 34,056 first-class runs and 52 hundreds for Glamorgan – and the man who led Glamorgan when they played at Lord's in the Gillette Cup final of 1977.

coaching, they not only made a fantastic team themselves but in turn were leading a fantastic team of players. The same core group – with one or two new additions, including a fired-up Waqar Younis – had simply moved on and up a couple of gears, ensuring the Sunday League wasn't a one-off.

To achieve promotion in the National League in 2001 and to go on to win the First Division in 2002 was another magnificent achievement. And in those two years the team was led by Steve James, with Adrian Dale deputizing on occasion in 2001 and Robert Croft in 2002, a reminder of that old Colts XI team photograph and how far those players – now senior stalwarts all – had come. The emergence of another generation of young talent over those two seasons was heartening to see and the establishment of the Academy under Steve Watkin in 2001 will ensure the conveyor belt continues to produce.

The Lord's final was a bit of a monkey on our backs. Having lost the 1988 Benson & Hedges Cup semi-final (the 'Maynard helmet' match), then watched on television with Tony Dilloway as Sussex recovered from 101-6 in the 1993 NatWest semi-final to dash the dreams we'd dared to dream, been humiliated by Warwickshire in a one-sided 1995 semi-final, finally suffering the 'infamous' Croft/Ilott semi-final against Essex when we posted 300+ and still lost, the victory over Surrey in the 2000 Benson & Hedges Cup semi-final led to an enormous outpouring of relief. Just as the players celebrated, so Tony and I hunted each another out for our own quiet celebration, an unspoken reminder to ourselves that the good times were worth it in the end. Okay, so Glamorgan had lost the final, but that'll come. At the time it was getting there that seemed more important as it was something we hadn't done for such a long time, falling at the final hurdle on four occasions.

Behind the scenes, the club has grown as well. Whereas before we didn't have a ground, the head lease of Sophia Gardens was acquired in the mid-1990s; whereas international cricket was the preserve of others, so Cardiff was added to the list a couple of years ago; whereas we didn't enjoy any facilities at all, so the first phase of the ground development was undertaken in 1998/99. The ground acquisition has brought its own challenges and county cricket in 2003 is a much more cut-throat world than it was back in 1986, both on and off the field. The ambition, which is still there, has made the business more difficult to manage but the turnaround on the field has been striking: three major trophies in ten years, a Lord's final, several semi-finals and a one-day second division title.

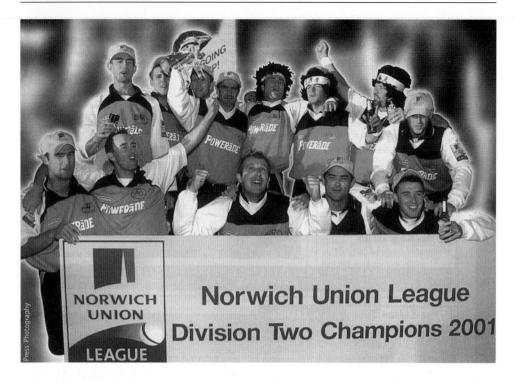

As far as 2002 is concerned, the reason for this book after all – well let's just say the memories aren't quite as hazy and I have the (lack of) nails to prove it! In many ways the key passage of play for me was the partnership between James and Maynard at Worcester. With iffy weather around, and behind on the Duckworth/Lewis method (and some of us can remember the halcyon days when games were decided by a system that didn't equate to an Einsteinian logarithmic conundrum!), those two set about rebuilding the innings such that we were ahead when the heavens opened. It might not be everyone's obvious memory of the campaign but for me, chauffering my daughters back from a day out in Hay-on-Wye with the wipers on full whack, I thought it was a crucial win (and memorable not just because I was 'done' by a speed camera in Bronllys on the same day!). We beat Worcestershire well in the return game, the day-nighter at Sophia Gardens in September, but the players were on a roll then and, without the win at New Road, it might have counted for so little. Sure, I enjoyed chewing my nails on the balcony at Canterbury with Darren Thomas, Owen Parkin, Roger Skyrme and an even-more-nervous-than-me Steve James, but although the feeling doesn't diminish with each trophy, 2002 couldn't really equate to the sheer exhilaration I felt at witnessing the title triumph on the same ground nine years earlier. But it capped a magnificent decade and it's been nothing less than a privilege to have been involved in such a successful era for the club. You can't sit back and assume it will keep repeating itself, though. The trick is to rebuild and go again and, crucially, the team now knows what it is to win.

2
1990 –
Year of the Bat

There will probably never be another summer like 1990 in English cricket. Batsmen gorged themselves as never before as 32 players hit double centuries and a record number of centuries were registered during the long, hot summer as bowlers up and down the country wilted under a hot sun and the daily grind of trying to extract life from some anodyne wickets and with a ball containing an experimental lower seam.

In all, ten players aggregated over 2,000 runs during the summer's run spree, and for one of these, Glamorgan's Hugh Morris, it was a season to savour, as the left-hander established new club records of 2,276 first-class runs and 10 centuries – the most any Glamorgan batsman had ever scored in a single season.

The 26-year-old opening batsman enjoyed a welcome return to form after a brief period as the club's captain, when the worries of leading a transitional side had weighed heavily on Hugh's mind, resulting in a loss of form. He also formed a highly productive and consistent opening partnership with Alan Butcher, and in all, the two left-handers shared ten century partnerships during 1990 and laid the foundations for many substantial totals.

Alan Butcher thrived on the responsibility as Glamorgan's captain, and his unbeaten 104 against Middlesex in the NatWest Trophy quarter-final epitomised his summer. On a sluggish and unresponsive surface, Glamorgan's top order, for once, found run-scoring difficult, but whilst wickets fell all around him, captain Butcher remained defiant, calmly countering the formidable Middlesex attack, and deservedly winning the Man of the Match award for his efforts as his side slumped to a resounding nine-wicket defeat.

It was a rare blip in a summer that saw Glamorgan take part in some truly remarkable Championship matches, none more so than at Abergavenny where Worcestershire left Glamorgan a seemingly improbable target of 495 runs on the final day, only to see the Welsh county come within two runs of recording a famous victory.

As so often in 1990, the Glamorgan run-chase was launched by a rollicking opening stand of 256 by Butcher and Morris. The cheap loss of Matthew Maynard and Tony Cottey seemed to have halted their progress, but Viv Richards then struck 43 off 18 balls to revive Welsh hopes, before Nigel Cowley and Robert Croft then added a blistering 124 in a mere 15 overs as Phil Neale, with a mix of frontline and occasional bowlers, kept Glamorgan interested in the run-chase.

As the game entered its final stages, the regular bowlers returned, and Cowley was caught behind off Ian Botham. But Robert Croft kept the run-chase going, and the

Hugh Morris.

target was down to 15 runs from the final over from Richard Illingworth. It was a tall order, but it looked as if Glamorgan might grab an amazing victory when Croft hit a huge six off the fourth delivery, and the ball sailed out of the ground and into the garden of an adjoining house. But the canny bowler, aiming wide of the leg stump, then stifled Croft's ambition with his final two deliveries, and Glamorgan ended just two runs short.

On the first day, Graeme Hick had become the youngest batsman in cricket history to score 50 first-class centuries, and his unbeaten 252 heralded the start of a run-fest that saw a total of 16 sixes and 249 fours being struck as bowlers on both sides were put to the sword. For 27-year-old seam bowler Mark Frost, 1990 was a rather cruel introduction to life on the Championship circuit. It was, after all, his first full season of county cricket, having failed to establish a regular place in the Surrey side. Despite the lifeless wickets and the low-seamed balls, the wholehearted seamer cheerfully kept running in for over after over, but at Abergavenny, the ball kept disappearing towards the boundary, or over the trees into the gardens of the adjoining houses. For a while as well, the ball rather followed him in the field, and as Nigel Cowley remembers, 'Frosty got a bit disorientated as the ball flew past him everywhere in the field, and he never seemed to be in the same place twice. Eventually I decided to help him by sticking a County rosette to the ground at third man and writing on it 'Frosty fields here'!'

The final month of a quite astonishing season saw both Hugh Morris and Alan Butcher pass the landmark of 2,000 runs in the season. Previously, only Gilbert Parkhouse and Javed Miandad had topped the 2,000-run mark, but 'Banners' and 'Butch' sailed past milestone after milestone and re-wrote the club's batting records.

Hugh reached the milestone of 2,000 runs during the County's match against Hampshire at Pontypridd in late August, yet his glut of runs was not quite enough to convince the English selectors, and more importantly captain Graham Gooch, that he was worthy of being chosen for the Test side and the winter tour of Australia. There were, not surprisingly, howls of protest about Hugh's omission and some of the Celtic anger was tempered at the end of the summer by news of Hugh's appointment as captain of the England A party to tour Pakistan. But even this did not stop several mischievous comments in the Press as to why Hugh had been overlooked. With some of the players treading the boards in Christmas pantomimes, the cartoon opposite shows the views of Gren, the cartoonist of the *South Wales Echo*, on why Hugh was not getting a chance on the big stage!

The batting records of Hugh Morris was just one of the feats established in 1990 as bowlers struggled up and down the country. Amongst the other curiosities during the long, hot summer was that Colin Metson, Glamorgan's wicketkeeper, did not record a single stumping in any of the Championship games, and it wasn't for the want of trying either as Glamorgan's front-line spinners, Robert Croft and Nigel Cowley, wheeled away for in excess of 700 overs.

1990 was the fourth year behind the timbers in Glamorgan colours for Metson, who had joined Glamorgan from Middlesex in 1987 following the decision by Terry Davies, the previous incumbent, to emigrate to Australia at the end of the previous summer.

CPM – It had been at first quite a culture shock for me to move away from Lord's where I had been Paul Downton's understudy. But I was not a first-team regular and I knew that I had to move if I was ever going to play first-team cricket. I had approaches from both Glamorgan and Somerset, before deciding on moving to South Wales. The first thing that I noticed was the difference in net facilities and no real headquarters to speak of. But there was a very friendly atmosphere within the club and I had plenty of time in which to settle in and try my best.

Middlesex had been a very successful side, but with Glamorgan at that time, there was never an expectation that they would win every game. Things started to change under Alan Butcher's captaincy. He was never afraid to leave even established players out of the team, and on occasions I was omitted for some of the one-day games as Martin Roberts was chosen instead as a wicketkeeper batsman. We were also very fortunate to have the services from 1990 of Viv Richards. We all knew that his best years were behind him, but even so he was still a marvellous player and opponents gave him so much respect. It was a wonderful opportunity for everyone at the club to learn from Viv, and we all enjoyed batting with him.

A cartoon from the *South Wales Echo,* showing what Gren thought the Radio Wales commentary team were talking about!

"I think Hugh Morris could have made the squad but his climbing of the beanstalk let him down"

Above: Ravi Shastri receives his County cap from Hugh Morris (left) and Alan Butcher (right).
Below left: Alan Butcher. *Below right:* Nigel Cowley.

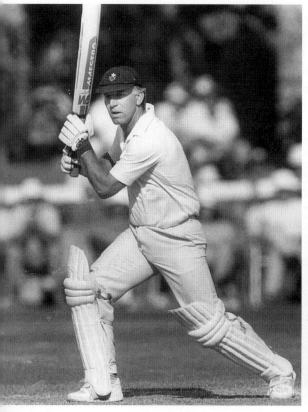

Mark Frost.

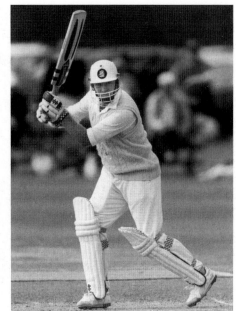

Hugh Morris.

Metson himself had a memorable partnership with Viv in the middle of June 1990 against Hampshire at Southampton, with the Glamorgan wicketkeeper standing almost in awe at the non-strikers' end as Viv played a truly remarkable innings, described by *Wisden* as 'a masterpiece of aggression and timing', and single-handedly guided his side to a four-wicket victory, chasing a target of 364 from a minimum of 102 overs on the final day.

CPM – *It was a good wicket to bat on, so the target was within our compass. But after Alan Butcher and Hugh Morris had given us a good start, we had a mid-innings slump, and by mid-afternoon it looked as if our chances of victory had gone. But Viv was still there and together with Nigel Cowley, over 150 runs were added before Cowley was out and I went to the crease. There were still around 60 or so runs needed, and just four wickets in hand. To make matters worse, it was starting to get dark, but Viv scented victory and I just hung around as he took us closer and closer to the target.*

There were still 12 runs needed from the final over, to be bowled by West Indian paceman Malcolm Marshall, but I was on strike. Viv was still confident that we could do it if I could quickly get him down the batting end. The first ball struck me on the pads and the ball flew to Raj Maru at first slip. But Viv was quickly out of the blocks at the other end, and we managed to scramble a leg bye. Then Viv hooked Marshall for four, drove the next ball for four and finished the game with another mighty six. It was exhilarating standing at the other end and watching Viv bat. He had so much time to play, even when Marshall was racing in – it was as if Viv knew exactly where each ball would be.

Above left and right: Colin Metson.

Hugh Morris sweeps the ball for another boundary.

Viv's brutal blows saw his side home with two balls to spare, and he left the field graciously acknowledging the handshakes from all of the Hampshire fielders, and then raised his bat as the crowd gave him a standing ovation having been enraptured by the sheer brilliance and fearless audacity of the Master Blaster. As Hampshire captain Mark Nicholas later recalled, 'I have never seen anybody play a better or more remarkable innings. He certainly left it late, but he did it and more power to his elbow. I sometimes wonder if playing against the likes of Malcolm Marshall pumps up someone like him. He blocked his way to 100 picking up the ones and twos, and then in the last four overs he hit it out of the ground. It was a wonderful innings – as fine an innings of its type as you would ever see.'

It was therefore no coincidence that the arrival of Viv Richards saw Glamorgan enjoy in 1990 their most successful summer for 20 years, with the club finishing in eighth place in the Championship, and reaching the quarter-final stages of both the knock-out one-day competitions. It also heralded the dawn of the most successful period in the Welsh county's history.

Nigel Cowley and Viv Richards leave Sophia Gardens after their match-winning partnership against Sussex in the 1990 NatWest Trophy.

3

Magnificent Maynard

Matthew Maynard burst onto the county scene in 1985, with the precocious nineteen year old scoring a magnificent century on his first-class debut as Glamorgan chased a target of 272 to beat Yorkshire on the final day of a rain-affected game at Swansea.

MPM – *I was batting at number 5 and came in at the healthy position of 120 for 3. In those days, Glamorgan were not used to winning, and we slid from 127 for 5 to 166 for 8. There was no pressure on me, so I decided to enjoy myself and play my natural game. By the time Phil North, the last man, was at the wicket, I had gone past fifty, and when I got to 84, Phil played out a maiden over – to a massive round of applause from the crowd who were willing me on to get a hundred.*

I realised that Phil was unlikely hang around for long, and that it was a case of now or never. But the field was set deep to offer me the single and get Phil on strike, and with virtually every fielder on the boundary, I realised that the only option was to go over the top. Phil Carrick, the experienced left-arm spinner, was bowling and after blocking his first ball, I went down the wicket to his second ball and sent it over the sightscreen. It was premeditated. The next ball I did the same. I didn't hit it right and it only just cleared long on. Carrick was a wily bowler, and I, a novice at nineteen, tried to read his mind. I decided that he would not expect me to come down the wicket a third time to him – so I did. The ball went a long way, and I had become the youngest Glamorgan player to hit a Championship century and the first to do so on his debut since Frank Pinch in 1921.

I realise now that I should have then taken a single off the fifth ball, but I didn't and was then out off the sixth trying to work a single, so it was a bit of a tame ending. My abiding memory afterwards was getting the handshakes of all the Glamorgan team in the dressing room, when in walked Geoff Boycott. He didn't speak to anyone else but came straight over to me and said 'Well played, lad.' It was a lovely gesture.

Matthew's remarkable debut may never have happened had it not been for some shrewd advice from Javed Miandad, Glamorgan's mercurial Pakistani batsman, whilst Matthew was having a trial in 1984 with the Welsh county.

MPM – *For a young player like me starting out, he was someone to look up to, and he had the attacking instincts which fired my game. After batting with him in a Second-XI match at Usk, Javed told me to work on my technique against the short ball, pointing out that I needed to get over it more. That winter I spent weeks in the nets having short balls bowled at me until I reached the point where I had ironed out the*

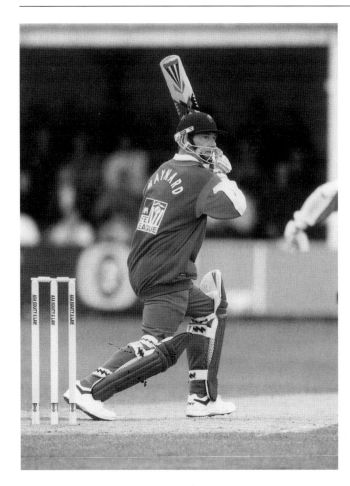

Matthew Maynard.

weakness Javed had spotted. It was an early glimpse for me of the value of an overseas player, one which extends beyond what he does with the bat or the ball. But for Javed, I may never have made it as a professional cricketer.

Matthew's hairstyles and hair colours may have changed many times since this explosive debut in 1985, but one thing about Matthew that has remained the same has been his audacious strokeplay. In 1986 he became the County's youngest-ever batsman to score a thousand runs – two years later, he made his Test debut against the West Indies, and was voted the country's Young Cricketer of the Year.

But there were a few low points as well, including the 1988 Benson & Hedges Cup semi-final against Derbyshire at Swansea, when Matthew's helmet fell off onto his stumps when he was batting against Michael Holding. The Glamorgan batting maestro appeared to be guiding his side to their first Lord's final since 1977, but after his freak dismissal, the Welsh resistance fell away.

MPM – *I was going so well, but then as I played a back-foot drive to Holding, my helmet fell off and rolled onto the stumps – something that had never happened before*

Javed Miandad.   Matthew Maynard.

or since! I kept the helmet and the newspaper photographs of the incident, and then in my Benefit Year, I raffled them for what turned out to be a quite tidy sum during a dinner at the Brangwyn Hall!

Even in the 1990s, there was still an impetuous streak in Matthew's strokeplay, but the presence of Viv Richards alongside him in the Glamorgan team helped Matthew turn a corner in his career.

MPM – *I believe that Viv has had the biggest influence of any individual person on the club since I started playing for Glamorgan. He gave us all direction, and stressed a positive attitude. Javed Miandad may have scored more runs for the club and broken more records than Viv, but he never won that number of games or helped us turn things around. Instead, Viv helped to change a team of good players who didn't really know how to win consistently into a winning unit with a desire to always win.*

There was a NatWest match in 1990 against Sussex at Cardiff when Paul Parker and Alan Wells were going well in a run-chase, and needed 100 or so off the final 20 overs. Heads started to drop after Ian Smith spilled a catch in the outfield, but Viv clapped his hands and encouraged Ian, saying 'Keep going, boy. Keep believing in yourself.' Soon afterwards, Smith took a good catch to get rid of Wells, and Viv got us all into a huddle and said 'Boys we can win this. Parker's starting to get tired, and just looking to hit boundaries. If we give him plenty of one's and two's, he'll soon be out.' And that's exactly what happened. Viv got rid of Parker, we got back into the game and ended up winning by 34 runs as Sussex collapsed. It was down to Viv that we turned things around and his positive mindset, whatever the scoreboard, rubbed off on me.

1991 saw Maynard in vintage form with the bat, especially amongst the august surroundings of Cheltenham College, as Glamorgan visited the Cotswold town for their Championship match with Gloucestershire. To the delight of the Festival crowd, Matthew gave a masterclass in the art of batting, recording centuries in both innings and mastering a lively Gloucestershire attack.

MPM – *It was a bit of a damp wicket and there were three wet patches on the track, all a yard or so in width. When the ball hit these, it did a bit, but I felt good throughout and remained positive in my outlook. Although the Gloucestershire bowlers put it in the right areas, I managed to see them off and was very proud of my achievement of a century in each innings.*

1991 was also the year when Steve Watkin made his debut in England colours, and deservedly won higher recognition after taking 92 wickets in 1989 and 65 in 1990. It was

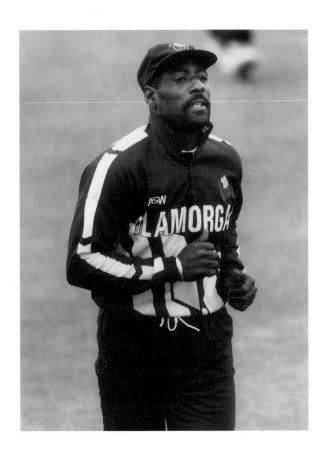

Viv Richards.

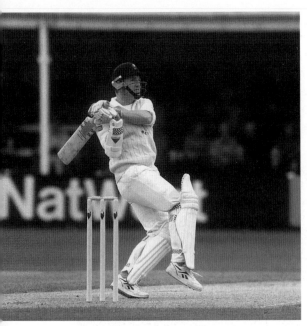
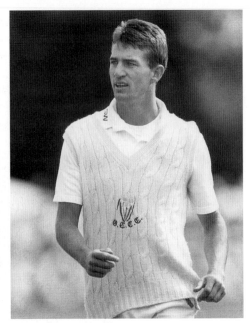

Above left: Hugh Morris batting at Cardiff during a career when he scored 18,520 first-class runs for the Welsh county. *Above right:* Steve Watkin – 861 first-class wickets for Glamorgan.

a handsome reward for the cheerful twenty-six-year-old fast-medium bowler, who had been one of the country's most consistent seam bowlers. Having made his Glamorgan debut in 1986, Steve recorded career-best figures of 8 for 59 against Warwickshire at Edgbaston in 1988, and the following year, he claimed 92 wickets to earn both his County cap as well as selection for the England A tour to East Africa and Zimbabwe in 1989/90.

Steve remained on the fringe of the Test side for the next couple of years, and in 1991 was called into the England side to play the West Indies at Headingley. He typically rose to the occasion with 3 for 38 in the second innings, as England recorded a morale-boosting victory. He retained his place for the Second Test at Lord's, as well as the winter tour to the West Indies with the A team.

SLW – Although 1989 was my most successful season, I think I had become a better bowler after 1990 when the seams on the ball were so low. I learnt then that I had to do something different to get wickets, with variations of line and length, and even a slower ball! However, I had nearly played for England in the Ashes series of 1989. When we played at The Oval, Alan Butcher, the Glamorgan captain, and Micky Stewart, the England coach, had a quick chat with me asking if I felt fit and strong enough to make it through a Test. In all honesty, I said I wasn't sure as I knew I was a bit stiff and sore, and was not bowling as well at the time as I knew I could. A few days later when we were playing against Kent, Micky Stewart rang me to say that the selectors had opted instead for Alan Igglesden.

I eventually won my first cap in 1991 against the West Indians at Headingley, along with other debutants Graeme Hick and Mark Ramprakash. I was a little bit tense and didn't really bowl very well there or at Lord's. Some people started to sum me up as a bowler who delivered good balls on juicy wickets, but not on flat ones. It was nice to prove them wrong at The Oval in 1993 and then to go on the West Indies tour. Overall though, I was disappointed not to get more opportunities with England. Although I was never on a losing Test side, I feel I was unproven at international level.

Steve Watkin in action.

4

All in a Spin

1991 also saw Hugh Morris finally get a chance in England colours, as the doughty left-hander played against the West Indies and Sri Lanka. In the Fifth Test at The Oval, Morris bravely fended off the hostile West Indian pace quartet to compile a composed 44 during an opening partnership of 112 with Graham Gooch. Yet at the end of the season, the selectors opted for other opening batsmen, with far inferior techniques and records, as Hugh was chosen instead to act as vice-captain of the A tour to the West Indies. Despite Hugh's disappointment at missing out on the main tour, there were signs that the Glamorgan club was on the up as Hugh was joined in the Caribbean by Steve Watkin and young off-spinner Robert Croft, another one of the young Welsh cricketers to be making an impact at county level.

Croft had made his Glamorgan debut in 1989, and the Welsh-speaking off-spinner soon stepped into the shoes hastily vacated by Rodney Ontong who had been forced into premature retirement after sustaining a severe knee injury in a car crash en route to a match in Northamptonshire in August 1988.

RDBC – 1989 was Rodney's Benefit Year, and the day before I made my debut at The Oval, Rodney drove me up to London for a Benefit Match. I suppose looking back now it was a funny twist of fate that the man whose place I took in the team should drive me all the way up to London for my first county match. It was a bit nerve-racking to be making my first-class debut surrounded by so many fine Glamorgan players, but there were a few young faces as well, and this helped me to settle in, and I soon realised what a great opportunity it was. I had a steady spell in Surrey's first innings and then claimed the wicket of Graham Thorpe in the second, when Alan Butcher held onto a catch running backwards at mid-on.

Croft's fine potential had also been recognised by the England selectors, who chose the uncapped spinner for the England A tour to the West Indies in 1991/92. Croft's first ball in international cricket, against West Indies A in St Vincent, saw the Welshman claim a wicket as Clayton Lambert was bowled behind his legs by a delivery from Croft who opted to start from around the wicket. 'It was just like any first ball of a spell', he recalls. 'You just hope to get it down there in the right area. Lambert didn't play a very good shot, it turned a bit and it bowled him. It certainly was a dream start.'

Croft subsequently came back from the Caribbean to enjoy his most productive summer to date, claiming 68 wickets in 1992, and bowling Glamorgan to a nail-biting victory against Warwickshire at Swansea. Defeat for the visitors had seemed almost inevitable when they slumped to 92 for 6 on the final day on a Swansea wicket offering

Robert Croft in action for Glamorgan.

the spinners great encouragement. But then Paul Smith and Dermot Reeve frustrated the Welsh county and their supporters for 30 overs after tea, until Reeve chipped Croft into Steve Watkin's hands at backward square leg.

Croft then picked up his sixth wicket of the innings as Booth edged him into the safe hands of Maynard at first slip, but then Allan Donald came out to offer more stubborn resistance with Smith. As Croft began the final over, it looked as though their victory chance had slipped away with Warwickshire on 171 for 8, but Donald edged Croft's third ball past Steve Watkin in the slips and down to the third-man boundary.

RDBC – I shouted to Steve to let the ball go for four so that I could continue bowling at Donald, because Smith had been in for a couple of hours. But Steve ignored my shouts, as he felt I was better off bowling to Smith because he had not faced spin for a few overs and he felt Donald was playing me comfortably.

Watkin's thoughts were fully vindicated as Smith jabbed the next ball into the hands of Steve James at forward short leg, and then last man Tim Munton froze at the vital moment, offering no shot to the penultimate delivery of the match, and umpire Graham Burgess raised his finger to give Glamorgan a well-deserved victory, while Croft left the field to a well-deserved standing ovation.

RDBC – It was a fantastic feeling to achieve this on a ground which has seen so many wonderful victories by Glamorgan, and to do it on the ground where I was brought up. Paul Smith had been playing so well all the way through, and I think the ball he edged into Steve's hands was the first one he had not hit in the middle of his bat. I then bowled an arm ball to Tim Munton, who just padded up right in front of middle stump, and it was a great feeling to see Graham Burgess' finger going up.

Robert Croft at the launch of the Glamorgan Short Legs with treasurer Richard Weston (left) and chairman David Morgan (right), plus three short legs!

Croft was one of several young players to emerge in 1992 and to win their County caps. In particular, Steve James and Adrian Dale each passed 1,000 runs for Glamorgan for the first time in their career. James took the opportunity in Alan Butcher's absence through injury to establish himself as Hugh Morris' opening partner, having completed his university studies at Swansea and Cambridge, where he had won cricket Blues in 1989 and 1990, as well as coming very, very close to winning one for rugby.

Adrian Dale had also graduated from Swansea University, and his big break in the Glamorgan team had come on the pre-season tour to Zimbabwe in 1990/91, when he recorded his maiden century. He subsequently moved up the batting order to number 3, and in 1992 he recorded an unbeaten 150 on a spiteful wicket at Trent Bridge. The summer also saw Adrian develop into a very handy medium-pace bowler, especially in one-day cricket.

Tony Cottey was the other young cricketer to win his spurs during the summer. The former soccer professional cemented a regular place in the Glamorgan side in 1992, and the 5ft 4in batsman proved that what he may have lacked in height, he more than made up for in heart, with his 141 against Kent at Canterbury proving to be a match-winning innings as Glamorgan won by 86 runs.

Two other young players to have their moments in 1992 were batsman David Hemp and bowler Darren Thomas, and at times there were as many as ten former Welsh Schools Internationals in the county side as Glamorgan reaped the rewards for its youth and schools cricket programme. But sadly, 1992 also proved to be the final season in Glamorgan colours for club captain Alan Butcher. He sustained a serious knee injury during the match against the Pakistani tourists, and was only able to appear in two Championship matches.

At the end of the season, Butcher left Glamorgan to accept a coaching post at Essex, and Mike Fatkin, the County's chief executive, paid him the following tribute in the *1993 Glamorgan Yearbook*. 'Since assuming the captaincy midway through the summer of 1989, Alan had moulded the side into a competitive unit, no longer regarded as the Championship whipping boys, and his record as a player alone since joining Glamorgan in 1987 bears comparison with any other during the equivalent period. Naturally, he continued to command the respect he and his position deserved off the field, and one felt enormous sympathy for him as he tried to cajole and encourage the team from the sidelines, all the while making a wholehearted, but ultimately fruitless effort to return to the fray.'

Robert Croft – bowling at Swansea.

Steve James strokes another four.

Butcher was not the only player to be on the sidelines during 1992, and as early as April, everyone on the staff, apart from reserve wicketkeeper Adrian Shaw, had taken the field. The treatment table used by Dean Conway, Glamorgan's popular and hugely well-respected physiotherapist, had already borne the weight of Messrs Barwick, Butcher, Croft, Cottey, Cowdrey, Dale, Metson and Richards, as they were treated for a wide variety of aches and pains, plus an assortment of dislocations and fractures.

In Butcher's absence, vice-captain Matthew Maynard enjoyed a taste of leadership during 1992. His team were thwarted by injuries and inclement weather, but morale, fuelled by the strong Welsh identity, remained high. This fine team spirit helped the side to enjoy a good run in the NatWest Trophy, and at Trent Bridge, seam bowler Steve Bastien hit the last ball of the game from England bowler Chris Lewis to the boundary to give his side a nail-biting victory.

SB – *I was determined to hit anything Chris Lewis pitched up to me. It had been very quiet in the dressing room because the game appeared to be slipping away from us, but I told Viv I would get the runs. I joined Steve Watkin at the wicket and we*

Adrian Dale.

Tony Cottey.

Father and son – Alan (right) and
Gary Butcher (below).

Steve Bastien – the hero of
Trent Bridge in 1992.

scrambled ten runs off the first five balls, so that we needed a single off the last ball. I was going to run like mad whether I hit it or not, but I saw the ball was up to me so I drove it. It was a fantastic feeling to see it speed to the boundary.

Bastien's efforts meant that Glamorgan secured a place in the quarter-finals against Northamptonshire at Swansea, and a capacity crowd of 11,000 thronged into the St Helen's ground, amidst much anticipation that 1992 would be the year when Glamorgan would break their one-day hoodoo and play in a Lord's final again. Their optimism seemed justified as Northants were restricted to 224 for 8 by some accurate Welsh bowling, but the Glamorgan batting collapsed, as ten wickets fell for just 103 runs and plans for a cup-final weekend in London were put on hold yet again.

It also seemed as if the weather gods were against Glamorgan in 1992, as a thunderstorm, almost of Biblical proportions, robbed them of a victory against Hampshire at Portsmouth. The Welsh county were just 14 runs away from their victory target when the heavens literally opened. No surprise then when at the end of the season, Matthew Maynard was asked by a journalist to reflect on the summer, his reply was 'I feel as though I've been through a tumbledrier!' 1992 was certainly a summer of highs and lows, yet within the space of twelve months, the club's fortunes had drastically changed for the better as the County won their first silverware for 24 years.

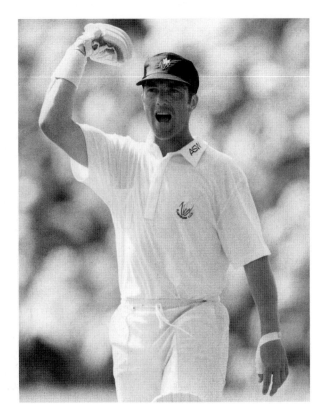

Matthew Maynard.

5

A Canterbury Tale

The foundations of a wonderful summer – the most successful for a quarter of a century – were laid during the winter months and in the spring of 1993. Perhaps the most important of all the pre-season events was a meeting at a plush London hotel attended by Glamorgan officials, a group of players and advertising executives from Andersen Consulting. The outcome was a reduced membership package, lowered from £45 to just £15, and a membership campaign, highlighting the club's Welsh identity.

Both were promoted during a walk around Wales, as players and office staff took to the road, visiting 60 venues, attending over a dozen sports forums, and arranging photo calls with local dignitaries and personalities. There were many smiles as the players, dressed in their dark blue and yellow Sunday League kit, mingled with the general public, signing autographs and handing out thousands of leaflets. Their hard work paid off, as Glamorgan's membership soared from 3,600 to 11,000 – the second highest in the country – and the club's income was boosted by £137,000.

There was also the incorporation of corporate business skills in the team's pre-season planning, with Hugh Morris and his team devising game plans and targets for everyone and for each player.

HM – *The new approach came in during our pre-season tour to Cape Town, as we held team meetings to set goals and targets. We focused in particular on running in between the wickets and fielding. It gave everyone a chance to chip in and it was the first time we had ever had goals for the whole summer. Each player also had a chance to discuss their role – it helped to take the pressure off, because everyone knew what was needed and what their job was.*

There were few changes though as far as the playing staff were concerned, with the only major acquisition being Roland Lefebvre, the thirty-year-old seam bowler who had spent the previous three years with Somerset. The Dutchman had previously produced some handy performances in one-day matches, as well as some good spells in domestic cricket in New Zealand, but he had become surplus to requirements at Taunton, and was looking for a fresh challenge. The signing of 'Roly' proved to be an inspired one by Hugh Morris and the cricket committee, as he brought an added element of control to the County's one-day attack.

CPM – *Roly was a little bit special because week in, week out, he was so reliable, rarely going for more than 15 or 20 in his opening overs. He was a very different bowler to Watty, who was quicker than you thought, always hitting the seam and*

Steve Watkin, Matthew Maynard and a giant daffodil in the streets of Abergavenny during the membership tour of Wales in 1993.

bowling straight. We always kept two overs of Roly up our sleeve, because he was wonderful at the death, bowling straight and full. He was also a fine fielder, with a very safe pair of hands. He always seemed to cling onto every chance and even with the easiest chance, he would end up diving on the floor and clinging on – to the delight of the crowd.

Throughout 1993, Lefebvre proved an ideal foil to Steve Watkin with the new ball, and the batsmen were already frustrated by the time the off-spin of Robert Croft or the off-cutters of Steve Barwick were introduced into the attack.

RDBC – *Steve Barwick was a key member of the attack, and his off-cutters were a vital asset, especially in these days when teams could have six men on the leg-side. It was a great feather in Steve's cap that some opponents called team meetings just to talk about how to play him!*

SRB – *It was great bowling with Roly or coming on after he had kept it tight. Batsmen were always trying to take chances against me and that was fine by me, as it meant I had a greater chance of getting them out.*

It all meant that barring injuries, Hugh Morris could call upon the services of a set of bowlers who contained the opposition, and in the spring of 1993, the Glamorgan captain duly started to plan ahead.

Action from the Glamorgan innings at Canterbury, as Kent's wicketkeeper Steve Marsh tries to run out Tony Cottey.

MPM – Hugh's policy was to bat first if we won the toss, confident that we had the bowlers to constrict the opposition, even if we were defending a small total. Eight of the twelve victories came after we had had first knock. On the four occasions when we batted second, the largest total we had to chase was 208 and with bowlers like Roly Lefebvre, Steve Barwick, Watty and Robert Croft, no one took liberties with us. Anyway, we always had Viv Richards and Adrian Dale as back-up. Hugh planned the campaign with military precision, operating his bowlers in pairs, and it worked before teams got used to it the following year.

There was one extra ingredient, namely the presence of Viv Richards, in his final summer of county cricket, eager to go out on a high and thank Glamorgan for the faith they had shown in him. There were early signs that the 'Master Blaster' meant business in the opening game of the summer – the friendly against Oxford University at The Parks. Fielding a full-strength side, Glamorgan romped to 463 by the close on the first day, with centuries from Hugh Morris and Matthew Maynard, plus a sublime 109 from Viv himself, reaching his hundred off 94 balls during a rollicking partnership of 233 in just 33 overs after tea with Maynard. At the end of the day's play, some of the undergraduate fielders even sprinted off into the dressing rooms to get their cameras so they could take a photograph of Viv walking off after his awesome knock.

It was then the turn of Sussex to be overwhelmed in the opening Championship match of the season at Cardiff, with the visitors capitulating after lunch on the final day as they chased 385 to win. Steve Watkin and Robert Croft shared 7 wickets between them as Sussex were out for 110 to leave Glamorgan cock-a-hoop after their opening four-day encounter. A fortnight later, they were celebrating a second win, as Derbyshire were beaten by 191 runs, thanks to impressive centuries from Hugh Morris and Matthew Maynard, plus another immaculate bowling performance from Steve Watkin.

The opening AXA Equity and Law League match against Derbyshire saw Steve Barwick take centre stage. The thirty-two year old had begun his county career back in 1981 as a fast-medium seamer, but in 1989 he switched to off-cutters, and like the legendary Don Shepherd before him, 'Baz' developed a miserly approach to bowling, as his subtle changes of pace tricked and teased county batsmen in both the long and short forms of the game.

In the game against Derbyshire, he recorded competition-best figures of 6 for 28, as Derbyshire lost their last eight wickets for just six runs in the space of 18 balls. But at the end of the day, there was little collectively for Glamorgan to smile about as their run-chase failed, with the Welsh county's batsmen faltering against some accurate Derbyshire bowling. The following weekend, Glamorgan went down to another defeat in the competition, this time at the hands of Northamptonshire, on their inaugural visit to Pentyrch.

The Parc-yr-Dwrlyn ground had been added to the County's calendar following concerns and a few difficulties when playing at Pontypridd in the previous few years. The club had a lucrative agreement with Taff-Ely Borough Council to stage matches inside their boundaries, but the change of venue did not alter Glamorgan's one-day fortunes as Northants successfully chased a target of 170 with two balls to spare.

By the start of June it seemed as if Glamorgan were destined to enjoy another fruitless season in one-day cricket, with the side at the foot of the Sunday table, and already out of the Benson &

Roland Lefebvre.

Above: Steve Barwick.
Right: Viv Richards.

Hedges tournament, after losing to Sussex at Cardiff. But the side maintained their good start in the Championship, claiming a third scalp at Middlesbrough where they beat Yorkshire by 121 runs. Centuries from Adrian Dale and Hugh Morris, plus 8 more wickets to Steve Watkin, set up the Welshmen's first Championship success on Yorkshire soil since 1970, and it took Glamorgan to the top of the county table at the start of June.

The Sunday League game at the Acklam Park ground also heralded a complete transformation in the club's one-day form, as they beat Yorkshire by 25 runs, thanks to a four-wicket spell by Steve Barwick supported by some tigerish fielding, especially by Viv Richards, who despite some taunts from the crowd, ran, caught and threw like a man half his age. The momentum was maintained the following weekend at The Oval where apart from Graham Thorpe, the Surrey batsmen offered little resistance to the Glamorgan attack, before Hugh Morris and Steve James quietly knocked off the 169 runs needed without being parted and created a new record partnership for the first wicket in the competition.

Buoyed by their rising fortunes in the one-day game and their lofty position in the Championship, Glamorgan headed to North Wales to play Durham at the Rhos-on-Sea ground in Colwyn Bay. A fine all-round team performance in the Championship match saw Durham lose by 113 runs, whilst in the Sunday League encounter, Adrian Dale took six wickets, including a hat-trick, as Glamorgan won by 166 runs – their largest-ever victory in the competition. Viv Richards also bowled several important spells in these one-day games with his unique mix of medium-pace cutters and floaters.

CPM – *Viv never really did much with the ball. He just bowled a mix of little swingers, straight ones, and added variety with the odd change of pace. Whenever he bowled he gave the batsmen a little stare and some opponents seemed almost afraid of him. He never went for many and was supported by good fielders in saving ones and twos on both sides of the wicket.*

In early July, Viv played another masterly innings in the Championship game against Middlesex at Cardiff. At the time, Glamorgan were in second place in the Championship table, with Middlesex in first place, and it turned out to be quite a remarkable contest at Sophia Gardens. Bat dominated ball on the first three days, as over 1,000 runs were rattled up on what appeared to be a most docile Cardiff wicket. It seemed as if Glamorgan were in the driving seat as their batsmen amassed 562 for 3, with Adrian Dale and Viv Richards adding an unbroken 425 for the fourth wicket – the highest-ever partnership in the history of the club.

Adrian Dale.

GLAMORGAN v MIDDLESEX / BRITANNIC ASSURANCE CH'SHIP

AT Sophia Gardens, Cardiff   ON   1/2/3/5 July 1993
TOSS WON BY   Glamorgan, who batted
BONUS POINTS: In the first 120 overs of the first innings, bonus points are available as follows: Batting – 200 runs = 1pt; 250 = 2pts; 300 = 3pts; 350 = 4pts. Bowling – 3wkts = 1pt; 5wkts = 2pts; 7wkts = 3pts; 9wkts = 4pts.

UMPIRES: J C Balderstone, V A Holder
SCORERS: B T Denning, H P H Sharp
HOURS OF PLAY: 1st, 2nd & 3rd days 11.00 – 6.30 (minimum 110 overs). 4th day 11.00 – 5.30 or 6.00 (minimum 102 overs). LUNCH: 1st, 2nd & 3rd days 1.15–1.55, 4th day 1.00–1.40. TEA: 1st, 2nd & 3rd days 4.10–4.30, 4th day 3.40–4.00

GLAMORGAN

		1st INNINGS		2nd INNINGS	Fall of Wkts	1stInn	2ndInn
1	S P JAMES	c Carr b Tufnell	42				
2	H MORRIS *	c Brown b Williams	27		1	50	1
3	A DALE	Not out	214		2	86	2
4	M P MAYNARD	c Gatting b Feltham	14		3	137	3
5	I V A RICHARDS	Not out	224		4		4
6	P A COTTEY				5		5
7	R D B CROFT				6		6
8	R P LEFEBVRE				7		7
9	C P METSON +				8		8
10	S L WATKIN				9		9
11	S R BARWICK						
	EXTRAS		41				
	TOTAL		562–3 dec.				

BOWLING	1st Innings				2nd Innings			
	O	M	R	W	O	M	R	W
WILLIAMS	26	5	85	1				
FRASER	33	3	127	0				
FELTHAM	27	4	117	1				
EMBUREY	35	5	102	0				
TUFNELL	45	8	114	1				

MIDDLESEX

		1st INNINGS		2nd INNINGS	Fall of Wkts	1stInn	2ndInn
1	D L HAYNES	LBW b Watkin	73				
2	M A ROSEBERRY				1	122	1
3	M W GATTING *				2		2
4	M R RAMPRAKASH				3		3
5	J D CARR				4		4
6	K R BROWN +				5		5
7	M A FELTHAM				6		6
8	J E EMBUREY				7		7
9	N F WILLIAMS				8		8
10	A R C FRASER				9		9
11	P C R TUFNELL						
	EXTRAS						
	TOTAL						

BOWLING	1st Innings				2nd Innings			
	O	M	R	W	O	M	R	W
WATKIN								
LEFEBVRE								
BARWICK								
CROFT								
DALE								

* CAPTAIN   + WICKETKEEPER

WE WOULD LIKE TO THANK OUR MATCH HOSTS TODAY CLEARWAY WATER TREATMENT LTD AND SOUTH GLAMORGAN COUNTY COUNCIL FOR THEIR SUPPORT AND ALSO OUR MATCHBALL SPONSORS BIRDS GARDEN CENTRE, COWBRIDGE

ASW and Glamorgan Cricket - A great Welsh partnership

The record-breaking partnership.

AD – We'd lost three early wickets so at first it was a rebuilding exercise, but everything just clicked and the runs started to flow. I remember one shot in particular when Angus Fraser bowled a widish ball that I hit to the boundary. Even though the ball was going for four, instinctively I set off up the wicket, only to see Viv still standing there, leaning on his bat handle. With a broad grin on his face he said 'Don't run youngster - you spoil the shot!' Later on, I think Viv got a bid fed up with me scampering quick singles, so he said to me with a wry smile, 'From now on we're only going run easy singles down to third man or fine leg, but God willing, we'll just be dealing with fours!' His words lifted my confidence and it was a great feeling to reach a double century matching him run for run. At the end of our stand, Viv made a big point of letting me walk off first, and afterwards he sat in the dressing room so proud of what we had both accomplished, but also so pleased that he had proved to the critics who had written him off, that he could still do the business against a quality attack. The partnership taught me many things, especially seeing Viv so determined not to give his wicket away, particularly against the part-time bowlers. My other abiding memory is a comment afterwards from Steve James. He told me he could never imagine what it would be like to bat long enough to score 200. Ironically, Steve's now scored more 200s for Glamorgan than anyone else!

Middlesex replied with 584, and when Glamorgan began their second innings shortly after noon on the final day, a draw seemed inevitable. However, in a little over 50 overs, the Welsh batsmen collapsed against the crafty left-arm spin of Phil Tufnell, whose career-best figures of 8 for 29 saw Middlesex to an easy 10-wicket win, which in the context of the final Championship standings, proved to be a crucial defeat for Hugh Morris' men.

SLW – We had gone into that match not wanting to lose and it got to a stage in the Middlesex innings where Mike Gatting came out to talk to Hugh to see if we wanted a game. A run-chase could have gone our way, but we declined Gatting's offer and opted instead for a draw. I suppose this game taught us always to be positive and to look for the win.

The day before, Glamorgan had maintained their rapid advance up the Sunday table with an emphatic 121-run victory over Middlesex, as the Welsh batsmen romped to 287 for 8 – their highest-ever total in the competition. Steve James led the way with a career best 94, but his record only lasted a week as he struck his maiden League century seven days later against Sussex at Llanelli. For the second week running, Steve shared a sizeable partnership with Hugh Morris to steer Glamorgan into a healthy position, before their accurate bowlers strangled the opposing batsmen once again and set up a win that took the Welsh county to the top of the Sunday table.

It had been a good week for the club as a few days before they had also reached the quarter-final of the NatWest Trophy, after recording a comprehensive second-round win over Durham at Cardiff. Their reward was a quarter-final tie against Worcestershire at Swansea, and a capacity crowd thronged into the St Helen's ground in mid-July, sensing that, at long last, this might actually be Glamorgan's year for a Lord's final. Any thoughts of a prompt start however, were dispelled by heavy overnight rain, but when play finally began at 2.15 p.m., the spectators were treated to a fine innings by Matthew Maynard, whose commanding 84 saw his side to a respectable total of 279 for 9.

Action from Glamorgan's match against Northamptonshire at Pentyrch.

Steve James and Hugh Morris share a word whilst batting at Cardiff.

In the 23 overs that remained that day, the Glamorgan bowlers gained the upper hand with as tight a display of bowling as many people had witnessed for a long time at the famous ground. Steve Watkin and Roland Lefebvre were in prime form, with the Dutchman conceding a mere 4 runs in his opening 8 over salvo that left Worcestershire reeling on 40-2 when stumps were drawn. The next morning, Lefebvre continued the good work by holding onto a vital catch to dismiss danger man Graeme Hick, and with the other Glamorgan bowlers not easing off, Worcestershire's resistance soon evaporated to give Glamorgan a 104-run win and a place in the semi-final for the first time since 1977.

Progress was also maintained in the County Championship with back-to-back victories away from home in the games at Old Trafford and Worcester. The victory against Lancashire was set up by an unbeaten, and most courageous, 138 from Steve James, whose first Championship hundred of the season was largely compiled after the doughty opener had fractured a finger after being struck on the glove by Phil de Freitas. For a while, it looked as if his bravery was in vain, as the damp Manchester microclimate led to time being lost. But on the final day, Lancashire were fed 235 runs in 12 overs, before Adrian Dale and Matthew Maynard each recorded half-centuries to see Glamorgan to their fifth Championship win of the summer.

The following week it became six, albeit in more nail-biting conditions against Worcestershire, as Glamorgan mounted another successful rain chase, this time in pursuit of 331 runs. When Adrian Dale was at the crease, a Glamorgan win seemed certain, but the loss of several wickets either side of tea, changed the complexion of the game. When Dale was finally out for 124, a Worcestershire win looked on the cards, especially as 10 runs were still needed, with the last pair of Glamorgan batsmen at the crease. But eighteen-year-old Darren Thomas, on his first Championship appearance of the summer, was unperturbed and the young tyro hit Richard Illingworth to the leg-side boundary to seal a Welsh win with three balls remaining.

The club's fine form in both the one-day and four-day games, plus the upswing in attendance, fuelled by the membership campaign, meant that there was a definite buzz about the side. Wherever Glamorgan were playing, there was a decent crowd and playing on so many outgrounds certainly helped the team.

PAC – *These games were an event for the locals and there was always a huge turnout, with a great atmosphere. Opponents were never quite sure what to expect either at some of the grounds, and together with the fantastic support, we had a 10-run start each time.*

With the team riding high in both forms of cricket, several players were enjoying purple patches of form. Hugh Morris had been the first batsman to reach 1,000 runs for the summer, Steve Watkin was amongst the country's leading wicket-takers, and Colin Metson had claimed more dismissals than any other wicket-keeper by the end of July. It was therefore a source of some misgiving that none of the Glamorgan players had been chosen so far for the Ashes series against Australia, and as the England side lurched from one defeat to another, some Welsh journalists launched quite pointed attacks on the England selectors.

The visit of the Australians at the end of July for the tourist match at Neath gave most of the Glamorgan players a chance to prove their worth in a game that was also a welcome break from the ding-dong Championship games and one-day

Steve Watkin follows through.

Roland Lefebvre.

contests. Billed locally as 'The Seventh Test', it saw Matthew Maynard carve his name in the cricket's record books by hitting a century before lunch on the second day – the first time any batsman had scored a hundred in a session against the Aussies since Ian Botham had done so in unforgettable style during the 1981 Ashes series.

Maynard raced to three figures off just 73 balls, and after his blistering efforts a few Welsh wags started wondering whether Glamorgan were going to record another famous victory against the tourists. But rain intervened on the final day to put paid to these flights of fancy, but it could not completely dampen Welsh spirits, following news that Matthew Maynard and Steve Watkin, who was being rested from the attack, had been called up for the Fifth Test at Edgbaston. The first few days of August were in fact a quite hectic time for Matthew, as his wife Sue was due to give birth.

MPM – *I didn't get much sleep the night before the first day of the Test. Nothing to do with staying up late or being affected by nerves – simply that Sue gave birth to our daughter Ceri at 3.40 a.m. in Llandough Hospital. I then marked the occasion by getting out for nought after coming in to bat before lunch. Not many people can say that they had a duck and a baby girl on the same day!*

With the Edgbaston wicket likely to assist the spinners, Middlesex's John Emburey had been hastily added to the England squad, and with Steve Watkin surplus to requirements at Edgbaston, the Glamorgan seamer returned to Cardiff to play against Warwickshire. He duly arrived with the visitors 9 wickets down, and had been on the field for a matter of seconds when he held onto a top edge from Keith Piper to give Adrian Dale career-best figures of 6 for 18. It proved to be quite a difficult batting surface, and after being set 138 to win, Glamorgan scrambled home with two wickets in hand after a plucky half-century from Hugh Morris gave his side the launching pad for a victory that maintained their Championship challenge.

Warwickshire were also beaten in the Sunday League encounter, so morale was sky high as the Glamorgan players made their way to Hove for the NatWest Trophy semi-final against Sussex on 11 August. A veritable army of Welsh supporters also made the journey down to the South Coast with everyone hoping that the contest would end with the Welsh side securing a fairytale Cup Final at Lord's in Viv Richards' last summer. The game instead, proved to be something of a nightmare.

Glamorgan did not post the commanding total their supporters had hoped, but Sussex then slumped to 110-6 after 44 overs in pursuit of a target of 221. The large throng of Welsh supporters were starting to clear their throats in readiness for a vocal celebration, but they never got beyond the first few splutters, as Sussex captain Alan Wells and Neil Lenham completely turned the game around with a match-winning partnership of 107.

PAC – When Lenham came in, we rather eased off, thinking the game was over. We took the pressure off and didn't really squeeze him. The fielders went back and we gave him too many singles early on. The bowling changes didn't work either, and as Lenham and Wells just kept going, it was a horrible feeling to sense the game slipping away from our grasp.

There was though one moment when Glamorgan might have broken the partnership, as Viv Richards tried to run out Wells. It was a close call as television replays showed Wells fractionally out of his ground, but these were the days before the referral of decisions to a third umpire, and the square-leg umpire adjudged Wells not out.

Wells duly guided his side home with four balls to spare, leaving the Glamorgan supporters rueing the fact that the side had not posted a larger total and had not had things go their way in the field. The Glamorgan players left the South Coast reflecting on what might have been, but they quickly bounced back and showed their character.

The defeat at Hove could have had major implications on previous Glamorgan teams, but not the Glamorgan side of 1993. The young colts from the previous few years had matured into an older and wiser unit, and after acquiring an almost addictive winning habit in the Sunday League, they were eager to return to winning ways.

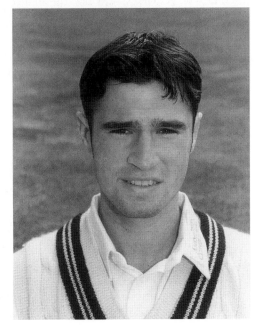

RDBC – The way we came back after the defeat at Hove showed our character, and in many ways, the game against Sussex was a turning point in all of our careers.

Darren Thomas.

Above: Hugh Morris relaxing at Swansea after another Sunday victory.

Below: Matthew Maynard.

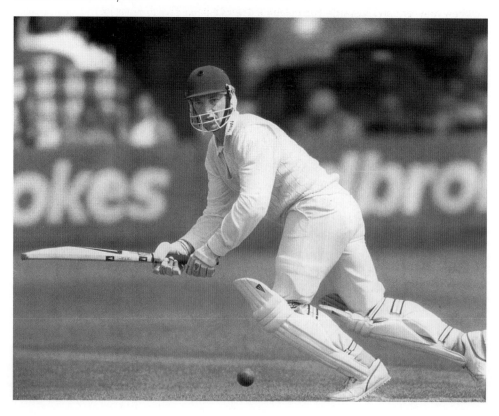

Matthew Maynard and Steve Watkin celebrate their England call-up at Neath.

This unified purpose was very evident as they swiftly put the disappointments of Hove behind them the following weekend at Leicester, and bounced back with an 8-run victory. The ground fielding was razor sharp and the bowling was exceptionally tight, with Roland Lefebvre conceding just 20 runs in his 10 overs. This followed a vital 27* from Roly, including 16 off the final over from Gordon Parsons, and thanks to the Dutchman's efforts, Glamorgan went back to the top of the Sunday table, ahead of Kent.

This dog-fight at the top of the table resumed the following weekend as Kent's narrow victory over Worcestershire boosted their run-rate and put them back in first place, despite Glamorgan's six-wicket win over Hampshire at Swansea. It could have been far worse for Hugh Morris' side, as they were without Matthew Maynard and Steve Watkin who had both been chosen in the England side for the Sixth Test at The Oval – the first time two Glamorgan players had appeared together in an England Test team. However, David Hemp and Steve Bastien both proved to be very able deputies, with Bastien bowling a disciplined new-ball spell with Lefebvre. Hugh Morris then played a fine captain's innings, and thanks to valiant support from the doughty Tony Cottey, Glamorgan won with fifteen balls to spare.

Seven days later a capacity crowd, in excess of 4,000, managed to shoehorn themselves into the compact Ebbw Vale ground for Glamorgan's next League encounter with Gloucestershire. They saw firstly Matthew Maynard, fresh from playing in a victorious England side at The Oval, play a disciplined innings of 69, before the Glamorgan bowlers, supported by some immaculate ground fielding, did their bit to frustrate the visiting batsmen, and set up Glamorgan's twelfth successive win in the competition to equal the record set by Middlesex in 1992.

Their efforts also set up a nail-biting end to the Sunday season, starting with a home contest with Essex at Sophia Gardens on 12 September. Kent, who Glamorgan were due to meet the following weekend in the final game of the season, had gone clear by two points after beating Northamptonshire the previous weekend, but they were not involved that weekend. 4,000 extra seats were installed at Cardiff in anticipation of a bumper crowd, but the contest turned into something of a damp squib, as rain forced the match to be abandoned with Essex on 7 for 2.

However, the two points allowed Glamorgan to move level with Kent on points. The outcome of the Championship had already been decided, with Middlesex confirmed as County Champions, despite Glamorgan recording victories over Gloucestershire and Essex, so as the ground staff mopped up the square at Cardiff, the County's fans started planning their pilgrimage to Canterbury for the head-to-head with Kent that would decide the outcome of the Sunday title the following weekend, which they hoped would mark Viv Richards' retirement with Glamorgan securing their first silverware since 1969.

The two counties were also engaged in a Championship encounter at the St Lawrence ground, and for a while it looked as if the tension was, for once, getting to

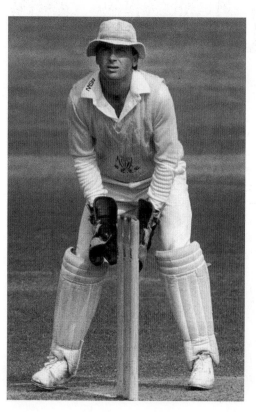

Hugh Morris' team, as Kent rattled up 524-6 after rain had washed out the first day's play. Glamorgan were then dismissed for 144, and even worse, Matthew Maynard ricked his neck and looked doubtful for the match on Sunday. Things seemed to be going wrong with Kent appearing to have stolen a vital psychological advantage. But on the Saturday, rather than enforcing the follow-on as everyone had expected, they opted to bat again, possibly to give some of their batsmen some practice before the Sunday match.

HM – *This decision actually worked against Kent, because we got a chance to experiment bowling against Trevor Ward and Matthew Fleming. We were worried that they might take our bowling apart on Sunday so we started*

Colin Metson.

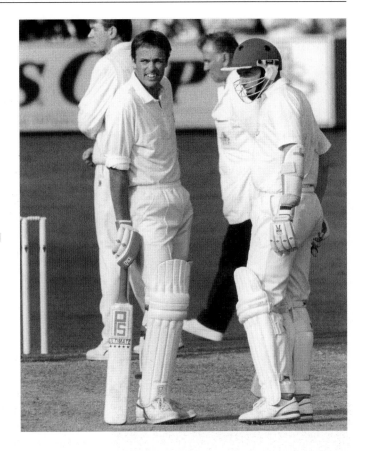

Roland Lefebvre (left) and
Robert Croft (right).

bowling the odd ball from a bit wider of the crease in order to change the angle and cramp them up. It worked and gave us a strategy that really helped the next day.

PAC – Viv was more than a little irate at Kent's decision to bat again, and he gathered us together after play that night and gave us a pep talk to the effect of, 'They will soon learn – mess with the game and the game will mess with you.' It gave us a huge lift before that game – to see Viv talking at the top of his voice, and with so much passion, saying about how much the next day meant to him, and saying that what had happened in the Championship match could not happen again. We were all a bit nervous because we didn't really know what it was all about because we had never been there before, but Viv's words helped to settle us down.

AD – A week or so before the Canterbury match I'd asked Viv what he thought our chances were of winning the League. He simply replied 'Don't worry, man - I know we are going to win. I've seen it' !

It seemed as if half of Wales descended on Canterbury on the morning of 19 September, and by seven o'clock in the morning there were already long queues of cars waiting outside the Canterbury ground.

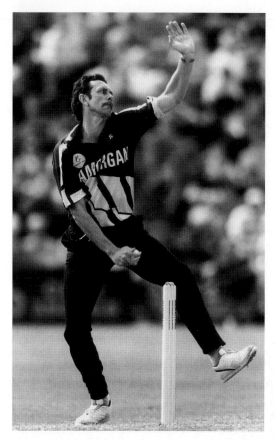

Steve Barwick in his delivery stride.

RDBC – *Thousands had travelled from Wales and I remember being stuck in a traffic jam driving to the ground. It was just solid, and the traffic wasn't moving. After being stuck there for some time, thinking about the game and what it meant, I started to worry that I'd miss the team warm-up. Then I spotted a guy walking past carrying a Welsh flag. I didn't think he was down in Kent shopping, but I double-checked that he was there for the game. I then asked him if he'd drive my car into the ground while I walked the rest of the way. He agreed – in hindsight, it was a pretty stupid thing to do, but I just wanted to get to the ground. I walked the rest of the way, surrounded by our fans. The atmosphere was great even at that stage.*

From early in the morning, the St Lawrence ground was buzzing with Welsh voices, and they were not disappointed as Glamorgan recorded a famous victory that even the most skilful of scriptwriters would have been hard pressed to devise for poignancy. The day had begun with good news for Matthew Maynard who was passed fit enough to play.

MPM – *I'd had neck spasms before, and I wouldn't have been able to play had the game been on the Saturday. But I had plenty of treatment, and by Sunday there was a bit more movement and less pain. I didn't want to let the boys down, but I backed myself at 80 per cent fit to do the business. As it turned out, it was little hindrance when I batted and it didn't restrict me at all in the field.*

Kent won the toss and on a slow, low pitch were given a brisk start by a few lusty blows from Matthew Fleming. But the Glamorgan bowlers kept the home batsmen in check, and Steve Watkin and Roland Lefebvre induced a late-order collapse that saw Kent falter and lose 5 wickets for 14 runs, leaving Glamorgan a target of 201.

HM – *It was quite a good wicket, and I think the atmosphere seemed to affect some of the Kent players rather than us. As wickets fell in their innings, I could see that several of their batsmen were quite nervous and thanks to our fine fielding and tight bowling, we kept Kent to a manageable total.*

Alan Igglesden soon raised Kent's spirits by removing Steve James with just 6 runs on the board, but Hugh Morris and Adrian Dale skilfully saw off the new-ball attack, adding 78 for the second wicket, before both fell attempting to force the pace. Viv Richards then came in to a spontaneous and emotional standing ovation from the crowd of 12,000. Soon afterwards, Matthew Maynard was trapped leg before, but Tony Cottey came in to keep Glamorgan's hopes alive.

PAC – I don't mind admitting that was the most nervous I've ever been before going out to bat. I just couldn't watch and it was torture waiting to go in. Fortunately, as soon as I got out there, the nerves went, and it was great batting with Viv. It was easy to come in and bat with him, as the opponents were so concerned about him that it took the pressure off me.

Even so, there were still a few heart-stopping moments, as Viv Richards was firstly hit on the chest by Duncan Spencer, Kent's Anglo-Australian pace bowler, and then the West Indian was caught off a bouncer. It looked as if Spencer had dealt a match-winning blow for his adopted county, but the umpire called no-ball, to a roar of delight from the Welsh supporters, and Richards remained at the crease. This was the defining moment of an enthralling contest as, from this point on, everything went in Glamorgan's favour, as Kentish spirits started to wilt.

CPM – As in our previous matches, Steve Barwick and I just sat at the back of the dressing room talking to each other. We'd done it all season and didn't want to change a winning pattern, but when Viv went out to bat, Baz and I went out onto the balcony to cheer him. But at the time, it was still touch and go whether or not we would get there, so Baz and I went back in and we only came out when there were about a dozen runs to win. By then the game was almost in the bag and we both wanted to share in the atmosphere.

Tony Cottey – the man who hit the winnings runs at Canterbury.

Above: Hugh Morris watches the rain fall at Cardiff in the Sunday match with Essex.
Below: Tony Cottey and Viv Richards sprint off the Canterbury ground after scoring the winning runs.

Viv Richards and Hugh Morris with the AXA and Equity Law Trophy.

The pair had added 60 in ten overs when Cottey hit the winning runs by top-edging Spencer high over the head of wicketkeeper Steve Marsh. As the ball sped to the unguarded boundary, the two Glamorgan batsmen ran off, punching the air with sheer delight. The champagne corks popped and emotions ran high in the Glamorgan dressing room. Viv himself was overcome with emotion and he was in tears as the team celebrated their first silverware since 1969.

RDBC – *Seeing him crying in our dressing room afterwards was a strange thing. Here was a guy who had done everything in the game, and to see him sitting there crying with joy, wearing a Glamorgan shirt, touched the hearts of all of us who were with him. He played for us for three seasons in all, and by the end of that time, he really wanted to win something with us. That was the mark of the man.*

PAC – *It was a great feeling to have won the game and it was something else to score the winning runs – albeit with a straight drive over the 'keeper's head! The win meant the world to us Glamorgan lads who had grown up together playing the game. But to see someone like Viv crying afterwards simply because it meant so much to him really brought home our achievements.*

Alan Jones and Hugh Morris as the champagne flows in the Canterbury dressing room.

Matthew Maynard batting against Derbyshire, watched by wicketkeeper Karl Krikken.

Glamorgan in the AXA Sunday League in 1993

18 May at Derby
Derbyshire 215 in 49.3 overs (P.D. Bowler 96, C.J. Adams 52, S.R. Barwick 6-28)
Glamorgan 212-8 in 50 overs (H. Morris 70, M.P. Maynard 69, F.A. Griffith 4-48)
Derbyshire won by 3 runs

23 May at Pentyrch
Glamorgan 169-9 in 50 overs (A. Dale 43, N.G.B. Cook 4-22, J.P. Taylor 3-32)
Northamptonshire 170-7 in 49.4 overs (R.J. Bailey 49, S.L. Watkin 2-28)
Northamptonshire won by 3 wickets

30 May at Taunton
Somerset *v*. Glamorgan: Match Abandoned

6 June at Middlesbrough
Glamorgan 208-9 in 50 overs (S.P. James 51, J.D. Batty 3-41)
Yorkshire 183 in 48.5 overs (R.J. Blakey 44, S.R. Barwick 4-27, I.V.A. Richards 3-21)
Glamorgan won by 35 runs

13 June at The Oval
Surrey 168 in 49 overs (G.P. Thorpe 75, S.L. Watkin 3-38, S.R. Barwick 2-22)
Glamorgan 169-0 in 46.2 overs (S.P. James 65*, H. Morris 98*)
Glamorgan won by 10 wickets

20 June at Colwyn Bay
Glamorgan 271-6 in 50 overs (M.P .Maynard 79, S.P. James 58, H. Morris 59)
Durham 105 in 40.1 overs (A. Dale 6-22, R.P. Lefebvre 2-22)
Glamorgan won by 166 runs

27 June at Swansea
Nottinghamshire 210 in 50 overs (C.L. Cairns 53, R.P. Lefebvre 3-31, I.V.A. Richards 2-12)
Glamorgan 211-7 in 48.5 overs (M.P .Maynard 72*, K.P. Evans 2-22)
Glamorgan won by 3 wickets

4 July at Sophia Gardens, Cardiff
Glamorgan 287-8 in 50 overs (S.P. James 94, A. Dale 61, P.N. Weekes 4-61)
Middlesex 166 in 48.3 overs (I.V.A. Richards 3-23, R.P. Lefebvre 2-10)
Glamorgan won by 121 runs

11 July at Llanelli
Glamorgan 269-8 in 50 overs (S.P. James 107, H. Morris 67, F.D. Stephenson 2-32)

Sussex 219 in 45.2 overs (A.P. Wells 51, P. Moores 56, A. Dale 3-38)
Glamorgan won by 50 runs

18 July at Old Trafford
Lancashire 167-9 in 50 overs (M.A. Atherton 64, S.L. Watkin 3-26)
Glamorgan 168-2 in 33.4 overs (H. Morris 87*, M.P. Maynard 72)
Glamorgan won by 8 wickets

25 July at Worcester
Glamorgan 259-7 in 50 overs (A. Dale 57, H. Morris 87, I.V.A. Richards 63)
Worcestershire 232 in 49.1 overs (T.S. Curtis 62, R.P. Lefebvre 3-38, I.V.A. Richards 2-27)
Glamorgan won by 27 runs

8 August at Neath
Warwickshire 163-8 in 50 overs (R.G. Twose 34, R.D.B. Croft 3-38)
Glamorgan 164-6 in 48 overs (A. Dale 54, H. Morris 46)
Glamorgan won by 4 wickets

15 August at Leicester
Glamorgan 228-7 in 50 overs (A. Dale 56, M.P. Maynard 54, J.M. Dakin 3-45)
Leicestershire 220-7 in 50 overs (J.J. Whitaker 117, S.R. Barwick 4-46)
Glamorgan won by 8 runs

22 August at Swansea
Hampshire 207-8 in 50 overs (R.A. Smith 75, A. Dale 3-25)
Glamorgan 209-4 in 47.3 overs (H. Morris 81, P.A. Cottey 75*)
Glamorgan won by 6 wickets

29 August at Ebbw Vale
Glamorgan 242-9 in 50 overs (M.P. Maynard 69, A.M. Smith 4-56)
Gloucestershire 211 in 47.5 overs (S.G. Hinks 62, S.L. Watkin 3-55, A. Dale 3-41)
Glamorgan won by 31 runs

12 September at Sophia Gardens, Cardiff
Essex 7-2 in 5 overs *v.* Glamorgan
No Result

19 September at Canterbury
Kent 200-9 in 50 overs (C.L. Hooper 60, S.L. Watkin 3-33)
Glamorgan 201-4 in 47.4 overs (H. Morris 67, I.V.A. Richards 46*)
Glamorgan won by 6 wickets

6

Life After Viv

The day after Glamorgan's wonderful win at Canterbury, Viv Richards played his final innings for Glamorgan. The club were certainly in a far healthier state compared with when he had signed for them, and as the great West Indian walked off the St Lawrence ground into the pavilion, he could take great pleasure from a job well done. He had arrived determined to bring success to the club.

ARB – *From the very start of our association, it was obvious that we had acquired a man with a mission. Having been unconvincing in his first innings for the club at Edgbaston in the Benson & Hedges Cup – hardly surprising, this, as he had only stepped off the plane from Antigua the previous day – he then produced an inspiring fielding performance, capped by a match-winning spell of bowling. This emphatic demonstration of his commitment and desire had a galvanising effect on the team's morale. It resulted in us playing cricket that was more confident and professional than I dared hope it might be.*

SPJ – *Viv's will to win rubbed off on everyone. Although he didn't do much coaching with the young players, he always said the right things out on the field. He was a forceful personality, and an absolute legend, and it was a great learning experience for a youngster like me just to be in the same side. I regret not having had more opportunities to bat with him.*

DLH – *Viv had a massive impact on the club, especially in the changing room. I was amazed at how calm he was when it came to the game itself. Nothing seemed to phase or bother him. He had a certain confidence that rubbed off on the majority of people who had the privilege to play in the same side as him. He simply played his natural game and encouraged everyone else to do the same.*

RDBC – *People's opinion of Glamorgan went up after Viv's signing. Many had previously considered Glamorgan to be a bit of an unfashionable county, but Viv's signing showed that we were a forward-thinking club, and were geared up to winning.*

Glamorgan's long-term plan had been that Viv Richards would be replaced from 1994 as the County's overseas player by a fast bowler who could bat. The decision appeared to be vindicated by the emergence of several home-grown batsmen, whilst Steve Watkin was desperately in need of a new-ball partner who could help to share the burden of the attack. After drawing up a shortlist, Glamorgan's choice was Ottis Gibson,

Viv Richards during his record-breaking innings against Middlesex at Cardiff in 1993. An exhausted Angus Fraser trudges back to his bowling mark.

a twenty-five-year-old Barbadian who was on the fringe of the West Indian team.

Gibson had experience of League cricket in Northern England, but he took time to adjust to the day-to-day demands that county cricket requires. Nevertheless, he still claimed 60 wickets, and also chipped in with 710 runs. But overall, 1994 was a quite disappointing season for Glamorgan. The euphoria of 1993 turned to frustration as the county slipped from third place in the Championship to the bottom of the table, in addition to enjoying a modest season in the one-day games.

Apart from Ottis Gibson, the team of 1994 was largely drawn from the same squad that had stood on the balcony at Canterbury the previous year. Some of the senior batsmen enjoyed a poor season in 1994, losing form for several vital weeks and with the batsmen's confidence at a low ebb, only Tony Cottey and David Hemp passed a thousand runs. An added factor was a knee injury to Hugh Morris, which necessitated the Glamorgan captain undergoing surgery in September. It was also Hugh's Benefit Year, and he was not the first, or the last in the county game, to suffer a lapse in form when organising fund-raising activities and functions.

The net result was that Glamorgan were rarely in a healthy position after the first innings of Championship games, and consequently were unable to dictate games as they had done so in the previous year. The one ray of sunshine was the emergence of David Hemp as a talented stroke-maker in the County's middle order.

The left-hander had made his County debut in 1991 following a fine career at Millfield School, and various Welsh junior teams. His assertive stroke play drew favourable

Thanks Viv – Hugh Morris and Jack Bannister make a special presentation to the 'master Blaster' at Cardiff in 1993.

Ottis Gibson (left) and
Roland Lefebvre (right).

David Hemp batting at Swansea in 1993.

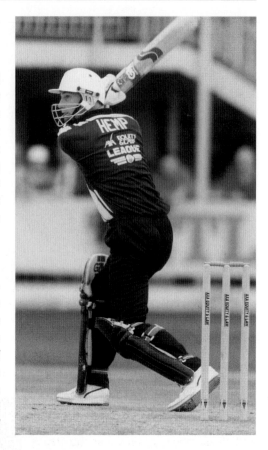

comparisons to that of the languid David Gower, and the highlight of 1994 for David was a century against the South Africans at Pontypridd – a hundred that led the tourists to rate the Glamorgan player as the most accomplished young batsman they met during the tour. It was no surprise therefore at the end of the season that Hemp was chosen on the England A tour to India and Bangladesh.

DLH – 1994 was a fantastic year for me, from scoring my first Championship hundred to the century against the South African tourists. The latter was special for two reasons – firstly because my wife is from South Africa and secondly, because I had ten of my South African friends watching the game on that particular day. Most players will tell the same story about the good seasons they have and it is fairly simple in that you score some runs and grow in confidence. For some reason, it does not seem to matter who you are playing against. The same certainly applied to me on that day. However, I remember the ball swinging around a lot early on, especially when Richard Snell was bowling. But I kept missing it, and before I knew it, I had hit a few boundaries and I was away. Thankfully, it proved to be my day.

Glamorgan's one-day form also slipped during 1994 in what proved to be an up and down summer in the various limited-overs games. They finished seventh in the Sunday League, after winning nine of the seventeen games, as their opponents discovered ways of disrupting both the bowler's accuracy, and the bowling pattern that had proved so useful to Hugh Morris' team the previous year.

But it was not all doom and gloom on the one-day front as the Welsh county reached the quarter-final of the NatWest competition. They overwhelmed Essex in the second round of the competition at Cardiff, thanks to half-centuries from Matthew Maynard, Tony Cottey and Robert Croft that took Glamorgan to 316-8, their highest-ever score in one-day cricket. Roland Lefebvre then stifled the visitor's top order, before Ottis Gibson claimed three victims in the middle order.

Thoughts that the side might rediscover their one-day form were extinguished at the end of July during the quarter-final against Surrey. Rain had washed out the first day's play, and after the wicket had sweated under the covers, Alec Stewart won a vital toss for the visitors. He had no hesitation in asking Glamorgan to bat first, and as expected Tony Murphy and West Indian Cameron Cuffy proved to be a handful in the damp and overcast conditions. Cuffy returned figures of 12-6-9-2, whilst Murphy had a career-best analysis of 12-3-26-6 as Glamorgan were dismissed for 161.

The Glamorgan bowlers did not have enough runs on the board in order to put any pressure on the talented Surrey batting line-up, and although Steve Barwick was in miserly mood, conceding just 17 runs in his 10 overs, the visitors reached their target with eleven overs to spare, and in effect, put an end to Glamorgan's season.

There was a realisation in the Glamorgan camp that 1994 had been a year of under-achievement, and Hugh Morris' team, especially the batsmen, were eager to make amends in 1995. The summer began in quite an encouraging way, with six consecutive wins in all competitions. This hinted at 1995 being a better season, but after victories in the opening pair of Championship matches, the County did not win another first-class contest until early September, and only moved two places up the table.

1995 turned into a summer of 'what might have been' as there were several near misses in Championship matches. Surrey's last pair hung on for a draw at The Oval after the loss of 22 overs through bad light on the previous evening, whilst Glamorgan ended up just two runs short of beating Kent in a run-chase at Tunbridge Wells.

The Glamorgan bowlers were also denied by the Gloucestershire tailenders in a remarkable game at Abergavenny that saw Andrew Symonds hit a world record number of sixes. The Anglo-Australian achieved the feat in an explosive innings of 254* that contained no fewer than 16 sixes, and all after having arrived at the crease with his side on 73-5. The twenty year old proceeded to take the game by the scruff of the neck, sharing a partnership of 213 with reserve wicketkeeper Reggie Williams.

Abergavenny may be one of the most delightful and picturesque of all of Glamorgan's grounds, but by common consent it's not one with the longest boundaries. Even so, many of Symonds' sledgehammer blows would have been sixes on the largest Test arena, with his record-breaking blow sailing high over the neatly mown outfield, over a row of hawthorns and into tennis courts on an adjoining recreation ground.

Hugh Morris.

Hugh Morris.

Roland Lefebvre.

Robert Croft.

Colin Metson.

He repeated some of these blows in Gloucestershire's second innings, and with the help of four more sixes in the second innings, he recorded the most number of sixes in a match. But despite his onslaught, the Glamorgan's bowlers stuck to their task in the second innings, and wickets started to fall, and Gloucestershire entered the final couple of overs with their last pair at the wicket. It looked as if Glamorgan would snatch a famous victory, but the final pair survived, even when from the final delivery, an edge from Viv Pike, their number 11 batsman, lobbed high over the head of Alistair Dalton at short-leg.

SLW – It was a very funny game, and without Symonds, who hit over 300 runs, and Srinath, who took 13 wickets in the match, Gloucestershire would not have been in the game. As always, the Abergavenny wicket was a flat one to bowl on. It was the first time we had really seen Symonds bat – he struck the ball well, and hit a few slogs. One of his 5 sixes off me saw him to the world record for the most number of sixes in a match, but I got my revenge as I trapped him leg before shortly afterwards!

The team's one-day form also fell away after an encouraging start. The team won seven out of their first eight games in the Sunday League, including a comprehensive nine-wicket defeat of Sussex at Cardiff, as Steve Barwick took 3-16 and Robert Croft 2-13 in their 8-overs allocation. In mid-June, Hugh Morris also scored a fine hundred in the victory over Middlesex at Colwyn Bay, and in the course of the innings went past Alan Jones's club record of 4,702 runs in the competition.

The following week, a nine-wicket demolition of Surrey maintained the team's quest of the Sunday title, but disaster struck in early July as Roland Lefebvre sustained a severe groin injury in the closing stages of the match against Durham at Swansea. The accurate Dutch bowler had to be assisted from the field after badly tearing a groin muscle, and his departure proved to be the turning point for the county's season as a whole. It left the Glamorgan attack without one of their key weapons, and opposing

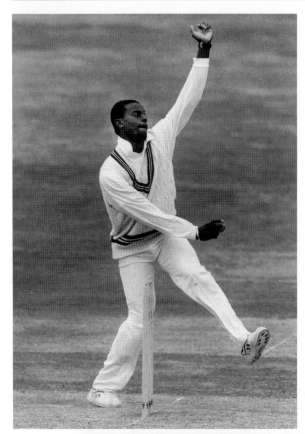

Hamish Anthony.

Hugh Morris sweeps a ball to the boundary.

Roland Lefebvre glances a ball off his legs.

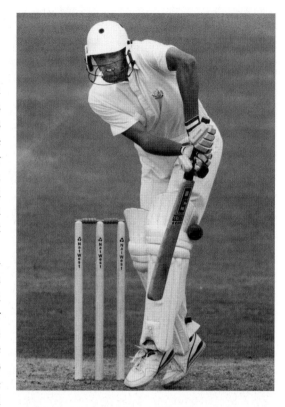

batsmen were able to play with greater freedom when Lefebvre was not in action. Durham duly won this contest off the last ball, and the Welsh side went on to record only one more victory in the competition in 1995, and that was achieved thanks to some batting heroics in a run-chase against Essex at Pontypridd.

Glamorgan were also handi-capped by the absence of Ottis Gibson for 1995. The all-rounder had been chosen for the West Indian tour of the UK, but confirmation of his selection did not occur until the late spring, and there was little time to sign a big name alternative. The county consequently re-signed Hamish Anthony, another West Indian all-rounder, who had played for the club in 1990. Anthony had a mixed season, but enjoyed a purple patch in the NatWest competition, taking 4-25 against Middlesex in the quarter-final at Cardiff.

The game with Middlesex also saw Colin Metson at his best behind the stumps, and the Glamorgan wicketkeeper took a stupendous catch as Keith Brown attempted a reverse-sweep against Robert Croft. Metson anticipated the stroke, so that by the time Brown played the stroke, he had moved across to where first slip would have been standing, before diving full length to his right to hold onto a remarkable catch that fittingly brought him the Man of the Match award.

CPM – *It was a premeditated gamble that worked as I knew Keith Brown liked to reverse-sweep, and I had tried it before in other games to similar batsmen. He began by playing orthodox sweeps, so I thought I would try it, as I knew he would soon start to reverse-sweep. Luckily, I was already going the right way when he played one and he got a good bat on it. There was sufficient height on it for me to get under it, and in fact, he couldn't really have hit it better for me to catch!*

Steve Watkin also bowled superbly in the match against Middlesex, taking 4-26, and this all helped to set up the prospect of a first Lord's final for eighteen long years, with a semi-final tie against Warwickshire at Cardiff. A massive crowd turned up at Sophia Gardens, hoping that the Lord's jinx that had hit the team at Hove in 1993 would not

Allan Donald and the Warwickshire team celebrate after the fall of another Glamorgan wicket.

occur again. But the Glamorgan faithful could barely believe their eyes as Glamorgan slumped to 77-8 at lunch, after winning the toss in fine sunshine, with the visitors almost beating Glamorgan at their own game.

RDBC – *To a large extent, I think that the Warwickshire side at that time based their success on copying our pattern of tight, aggressive fielding and bowling in partnerships. Dermot Reeve, their captain, had told me that he thought these were our two great strengths from 1993, and these were the two areas he focused on when he was leading Warwickshire.*

The Glamorgan innings never gained any sort of momentum, and at first, didn't get the rub of the green as Hugh Morris was adjudged by the umpire to have edged a ball from Tim Munton to the 'keeper. But they only had themselves to blame as both Matthew Maynard and David Hemp were run out attempting singles to Trevor Penney, the Zimbabwean fielder, who was one of the sharpest men in the covers and had a reputation of hitting the stumps more often than not when fielding. Even with just one stump to aim at, Penney proved his razor-sharp abilities, as Glamorgan were dismissed for a paltry 87. By 3.30 p.m. Warwickshire's batsmen had scored the runs they needed to see the Midlands county to their third successive NatWest final.

PAC – *Warwickshire were a fine all-round team who knew how to put the pressure on, and they made us forget what we were good at. At one stage, it felt as if we just didn't know where the next run was coming from. We were frustrated, the crowd was frustrated and some poor shots were played. We were all gutted afterwards and then going to field after our innings was the most embarrassing moment of my playing career with Glamorgan.*

HM – *That was our worst performance for three years and we couldn't have done it at a worse time. We had spent days talking about how we were going to approach the game and watched videos of the match at Canterbury when we won the Sunday League. We also had the slow wicket we wanted and we had the advantage of winning the toss, but at the end of the day, we did not make the most of it and produced a very poor batting performance. The standards we had set ourselves over the previous three years and a game plan we had talked about the previous evening had deserted us just when they mattered most. The players were distraught, the supporters were disillusioned and everybody felt numb. Expectations had increased dramatically over the last couple of years, making disappointments that much harder to take.*

Steve James was one Glamorgan batsman who could look back with a smile on the summer of 1995 as he scored a record 815 runs in the Sunday competition, including eight half-centuries, and struck a career-best 230* in the Championship match at Leicester. But the season had begun in the worst possible way for the twenty-seven year old, who sustained a leg injury and missed the Welsh county's pre-season tour. With Glamorgan's selectors likely to only choose five specialist batsmen, James looked as though he would miss out. But an injury to Hugh Morris at the start of the season, led to James' inclusion for the first Benson & Hedges Cup match. He responded with a match-winning 82 – the first of four consecutive half-centuries in the competition that helped to cement a place for 'Sid' in the Glamorgan side.

SPJ – *1995 was certainly a breakthrough year for me and all ironically after I had missed the pre-season tour and had been told by Hugh that I was unlikely to figure in the starting line-up for the opening games. Then Hugh was injured, I got a few runs and secured a regular place in the team. My double hundred against Leicestershire was the turning point of my career, and all after going back to basics with my technique. In the previous couple of years, I had become a bit too wrapped up on fiddling with my stance and pick-up. So in my dark days after missing out on the pre-season tour, I decided to make things simple and go back to basics.*

However, other batsmen, including David Hemp and Adrian Dale had a lean spell, and with the captaincy weighing on his mind, Hugh Morris was not as productive as he might have wished. There had been flickers of form in 1995, but Glamorgan as a unit were not functioning on all cylinders, and as the season entered its final month, Hugh called it a day as the club's captain.

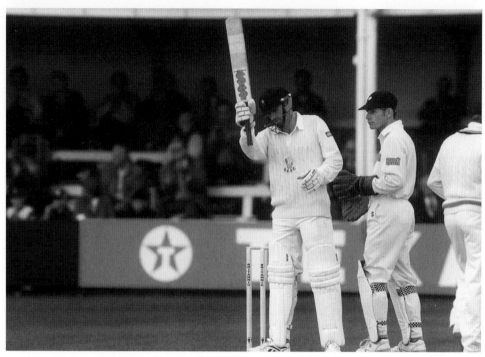

Steve James acknowledges the crowd's applause after reaching fifty against Yorkshire.

HM – *I had enjoyed doing the job and had seen the team make great headway to become one of the best one-day sides in the country. Our Championship form of 1993 had highlighted our potential, and showed that we were capable of getting into a winning position more often. From a personal point of view, I was not performing at the top of the order. I felt it would be best for the side if I stood down. In many ways, it was one of the hardest decisions I had to make. At the time, I felt that it was the right one and what happened over the next few years, proved it was right.*

7

Matthew Takes Charge

In the autumn of 1995, Matthew Maynard was appointed as Hugh Morris' successor to the Glamorgan captaincy as the Welsh county attempted to put aside the disappointments of the previous few seasons and collectively build on the progress that individuals had made since the Sunday League success in 1993.

Matthew immediately set himself the target of leading Glamorgan to six Championship victories and finding consistent form in the one-day games. The fact that the club achieved the former and reached the quarter-final of the Benson & Hedges was a sign that headway had been made under their new leader, and they might have achieved even more headway had the club not been hit by two early setbacks. The first came even before a ball had been bowled as it was confirmed that Roland Lefebvre would have to retire after his serious injury the previous summer.

Then in April, Ottis Gibson arrived in the UK carrying a groin injury that eventually needed a hernia operation at the end of May. The West Indian was only able to play in nine first-class games, and although he bowled 254 overs, he was rarely able to steam in off his full run. However, Gibson showed that he had not lost his abilities with the bat, and in early August against Leicestershire at Swansea, he added a club record 211 for the seventh wicket with the redoubtable Tony Cottey.

Gibson also played a match-winning innings in the AXA game against Gloucestershire at Bristol after Glamorgan had been inserted and slipped to 56 for 6. The West Indian helped to turn the game around, together with valiant support from young batsman Alun Evans, and reserve wicketkeeper Adrian Shaw. Their efforts saw Glamorgan to a more respectable 196 for 7, and then Gloucestershire were dismissed for 102 as Gary Butcher, another young player, made his mark by taking 4 wickets.

GPB – *It was nice to have my father around when I first came to Glamorgan, and he used to come and watch me play for the seconds and pass on some useful advice. But it became easier for me when Dad retired and went to coach Essex. I had always been referred to as Alan's son, rather than as a player in my own right. It's always in the back of your mind that people are saying you are only there because of your father – that sort of thing really wound me up.*

This was one of seven victories for Maynard's team in the AXA League, but they struggled for consistency in the competition

MPM – *We badly missed Roland Lefebvre and the 5-4 legside field hindered Steve Barwick and Robert Croft. But what was hard to understand was that we could be*

Matthew Maynard.

brilliant one week and awful the next.

Injuries, and the absence of Maynard on One-Day International duty with England, also meant that a settled side was an elusive dream. They also tinkered with the batting order, and in the search for the right formula, Robert Croft had a spell up the order as a pinch-hitter. Several new faces were drafted in, and amongst those to rise to the challenge was Adrian Shaw, the popular Second XI wicketkeeper, who also got a run in the Championship side towards the end of the season. The former Neath RFC three-quarter showed great promise with both the gloves and the bat, whilst his chirpy, vocal support from behind the stumps added a new dimension to Glamorgan's fielding.

Earlier in the season, Glamorgan had progressed to the quarter-final stages of the Benson & Hedges Cup after winning four of their five games in the zonal rounds of the competition. The season began with victories over Essex and the British Universities, before Maynard's side lost to Somerset in a rain-affected contest with Somerset. They soon returned to winning ways in the next game at Lord's, where Maynard led by example with a truly awesome display of batting as his side chased a target of 264 against Middlesex. His unbeaten 151 saw his team to a six-wicket victory with seven balls to spare.

Maynard's brilliance meant that Glamorgan travelled to play Kent knowing that they had to win to qualify for the quarter-final stages. Their journey to the St Lawrence ground in Canterbury rekindled memories of 1993, and Steve Watkin lifted his team's spirits as he took the first four wickets at a cost of five runs in 21 balls after Kent had opted to bat first.

They subsequently recovered thanks to their West Indian all-rounder Carl Hooper, but even so, the target of 211 did not appear to be too daunting. However, there was an added dimension, as Glamorgan needed to improve their own run-rate in order to reach the quarter-finals, and Glamorgan needed to reach their target within 38.4 overs. Hugh Morris then played another brilliant innings, adding 181 in 25 overs with Steve James and hitting an awesome century from just 68 balls to see the Welsh side to a home quarter-final tie with Warwickshire.

Matt and Hugh, modelling a new line in Glamorgan leisurewear.

Ottis Gibson and the Glamorgan side celebrate as the West Indian takes another wicket.

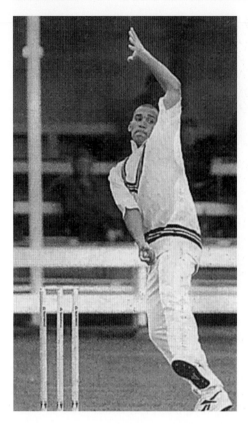

Left: Gary Butcher bowling at Cardiff.

Opposite: Adrian Shaw batting at Abergavenny.

SPJ – That was probably the best one-day innings I ever saw Hugh play. He was on fire and completely took the attack apart. Wherever they bowled, Hugh just smashed it. Going for the runs inside 38 overs, rather than going for the win over the full 50 overs, was a high risk strategy, and it could easily have back-fired had we lost early wickets. But Hugh was magnificent and saw us through.

After the disappointments of their 1995 NatWest Trophy contest with Warwickshire, Matthew Maynard and his men were eager to set the record straight, and after being put in Warwickshire stuttered to 151-6. However, the Glamorgan bowlers could not dislodge Dominic Ostler who proceeded to play a patient and invaluable innings of 85 to guide his side to a total of 239 that on the slow Cardiff wicket was quite a challenging one.

It seemed a very far off target as Glamorgan's top order struggled against the Warwickshire seamers, and at 80-5, Warwickshire looked destined for a comfortable victory. But Glamorgan duly recovered, thanks to a spirited sixth-wicket partnership between Matthew Maynard and Ottis Gibson. They had added 136 runs and had put their side back into the match, with the equation down to 29 runs from the final six overs, when the partnership was broken. A dramatic collapse then occurred, as the last 5 wickets fell for just 11 runs as another chance of an appearance in a Lord's final disappeared from Glamorgan's grasp.

But the clouds of disappointment were not as gloomy as the previous year, especially as 1996 witnessed a return to form for several batsmen including Tony Cottey, who scored a fine 203 against Leicestershire at Swansea and shared a record seventh partnership of 211 with Ottis Gibson.

PAC – St Helen's was my home ground and it was great to score a double hundred on my home track, and where I had started going when I was five. I had played in the Swansea seconds aged twelve, and when I was thirteen I had played my first game for Swansea's first team. Even better, my parents were there watching me bat against

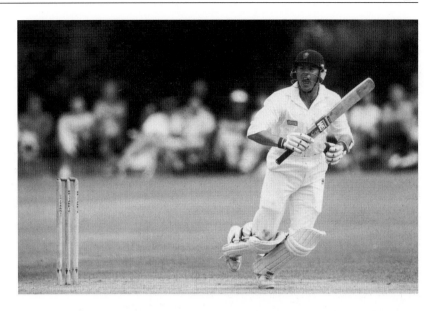

Leicestershire who that year were County Champions. It was hard work against their attack, but it was one of my best, and most satisfying, innings.

In all, 23 centuries were recorded during 1996 as Steve James, Hugh Morris, Tony Cottey and Matthew Maynard all exceeded 1,500 runs in first-class cricket. For Hugh Morris in particular, 1996 saw a return to form for the plucky opening batsman who began the summer with an unbeaten 202 in the opening Championship fixture against Yorkshire at Cardiff.

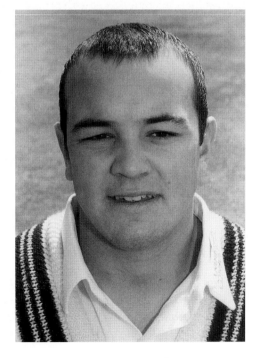

His opening partner Steve James also had a season to savour, finishing with an aggregate of 1,766 runs, which was only surpassed by Graham Gooch of Essex and England. The match with Nottingham-shire at Worksop saw James reach another personal best with 235 in a marathon eight and a quarter innings that gave his team an invaluable lead of 118 and provided the platform they needed on the final day from which they could put pressure on the Nottinghamshire batsmen. His efforts bore fruit after lunch on the final day as Ottis Gibson and left-

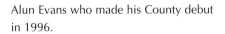
Alun Evans who made his County debut in 1996.

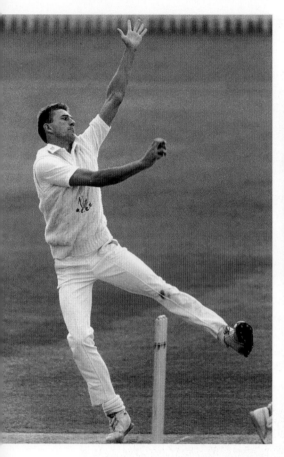

Steve Watkin.

Neil Kendrick.

arm spinner Neil Kendrick instigated a dramatic collapse as the final 5 wickets fell for just 9 runs. Hugh Morris then calmly guided Glamorgan to their target of 124 with 8 wickets in hand and a well-deserved victory for the Welsh side.

SPJ – I had worked hard on my technique before the season, and my reward was the double hundred at Worksop. I used to get out a lot in the slip area because I liked playing the ball through third man. I had changed my style to play more in front of the wicket, but I think confidence had a lot to do with my good form. It also helped playing with Hugh on a regular basis. We got to know each other's game so well and our understanding simply got better and better. We were also an ideal pairing with our left-right combination. Bowlers do not like that because it means they have to work even harder to find their line and can easily get thrown out of their rhythm.

But not every Glamorgan batsmen enjoyed a fruitful season in 1996, as David Hemp sustained a frightening injury at Fenner's during the Benson & Hedges Cup match against the British Universities at the end of April. Hemp collided in the field with Hugh Morris, as the two Glamorgan fielders ran towards each other in an attempt to catch a top edge from Gul Khan. The sickening collision left Hemp with four broken ribs and a punctured lung, and he was out of action for over two months.

DLH – *I certainly don't have fond memories of that game, but I guess that's life. What I do remember is Crofty bowling and the ball being hit out towards the deep mid-wicket boundary. I had no idea Hugh was anywhere near me, and as I caught the ball we collided. The next thing I knew I was lying on the ground in a lot of pain! To make matters worse, I dropped the ball as well! Unfortunately though, it did make the season a very difficult one, as I was sidelined for so long.*

In Hemp's absence, other players established themselves in the top three, and with his contract up for renewal at the end of the season, Hemp agreed to join Warwickshire for 1997.

Robert Croft had much more to smile about in 1996 as the jaunty off-spinner made his England debut in the final Test of the series with Pakistan at The Oval. Together with Steve Watkin, 'Crofty' had been the bulwark of the Glamorgan attack for several years, and in the eyes of many Welsh supporters, his elevation was long overdue after several summers of accurate and restrictive bowling in both the short and long forms of the county game.

In mid-June, he exploited a dry Swansea wicket to spin Glamorgan to a 173-run victory over Somerset, returning second innings figures of 6-78. The following month

Tony Cottey.

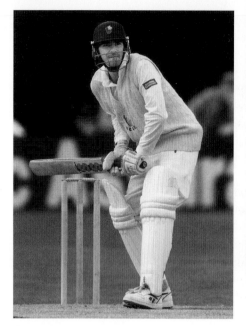

Steve James.

Matthew Maynard.

Hugh Morris.

David Hemp fully recovered after his nasty injury at Cambridge.

he further advanced his claims for a Test cap by taking 5-47 on the final day of the Championship match against Lancashire at Cardiff, as Glamorgan recorded another encouraging victory.

RDBC – *It was fantastic to get the call-up as I felt I had been OK for a couple of years. It was a great experience to make my debut at The Oval – it's been a bit of a lucky ground for me, as it was there that I made my first-class debut. Playing Test cricket was a massive step up from county matches, especially the intensity of the games. The Pakistanis had two left-handed openers, and I felt I bowled well to them. I had two lbw shouts turned down before Aamir Sohail was caught on the drive by Dominic Cork. I was delighted to get my first Test wicket, especially as I didn't want to be remembered as the man who failed to get a Test wicket!*

Between them Robert Croft and Steve Watkin bowled almost 1,400 overs in the Championship and shared 130 wickets between them. The next most successful bowler in the County's averages was young all-rounder Gary Butcher with 20 wickets at a cost of 35.80. If ever a statistic was needed to highlight the need for another top-quality bowler, this was the one for the cricket committee to mull over as they met during 1996 to plan the next move in the club's renaissance.

8

County Champions

After their slide down the Championship table and their yo-yo form in one-day cricket, it was widely felt that Glamorgan needed a high-profile overseas player to reignite the spark in the club in the way that Viv Richards had done in the early 1990s. In the middle of 1996, Mike Fatkin and Matthew Maynard made contact with Jonathan Barnett, a leading player's agent, to see which high-profile players might be available for 1997. A top-quality overseas bowler was at the top of their shopping list, and the outcome of the meeting in London with Barnett was the signing of Waqar Younis.

The Pakistani had a fine Test record and was one of the world's finest exponents of reverse swing. He had also played with some success for Surrey, taking 232 wickets in three seasons of Championship cricket between 1990 and 1993, and in 1991, he had claimed 113 wickets at just 14 runs apiece. Waqar was now very interested in resuming his county career, and despite a lucrative offer from Surrey to re-join them, plus approaches from three other counties, he liked the idea of living and playing well away from London and the glare of publicity that it brought.

MPM – *After talking to him for only a few minutes, I knew he was the right man. I told him about the enthusiasm, the new air and spirit of determination in the camp, and he was as enthusiastic as me. I was really delighted when Mike Fatkin and myself returned by train from London after signing Waqar. I was firmly of the opinion that we had finally put the last piece into the jigsaw – a pace bowler who added an extra dimension into our attack and someone who could run through sides on even the most unhelpful of surfaces.*

SPJ – *I was in Cardiff having a drink with Adrian Dale when Matthew told us that we had signed Waqar. It was amazing news as it seemed that he was the sort of player other counties always got – a really fast and devastating bowler of that class was what we had missed for several years. I was so pleased we had signed him.*

ADS – *When we gathered at the start of the 1997 season, there was a real buzz in the club. We had had some good overseas players before, but Waqar was something different. Psychologically, he gave us a huge lift and it was a great boost having him around.*

Waqar was also upbeat about his summer in Wales, as he said in his interviews on arriving in readiness for his first game. 'I wanted to get away from London, and Glamorgan is the right place to be. I've enjoyed playing against Glamorgan in the past,

Matthew Maynard lifts the Championship trophy on the balcony at Taunton after Glamorgan's victory over Somerset.

it's a good County and Cardiff is a beautiful place to play. I know how much the club wants to succeed and I will be giving my best to help Glamorgan win trophies – and I am sure we will do that.'

However, it was another pace bowler who struck the first blow, quite literally, as Allan Donald, the South African pace-man, struck Hugh Morris with a nasty blow on the helmet during Glamorgan's opening Championship match against Warwickshire at Cardiff. However, it came at the time when Hugh was unbeaten on 233 with Glamorgan cruising towards a lead of 400 over Warwickshire and seemingly exorcising all of the bad memories that the visitors had caused in their previous visits to the Cardiff ground.

HM – *I had just hit Donald for a couple of boundaries and he didn't like being made to look a fool. The ball that hit me was only a little bit short and I ducked thinking it was going over me. But when I saw it, I instinctively turned away and it hit me on the part where the grille joins the helmet behind the ear. Half an inch lower and it would have got me full on the base of the skull. I have been hit a few times on the head in the past, but never as hard as that. If it had not been for the helmet I dread to think what would have happened.*

Hugh was carried off the field on a stretcher, and went to hospital for an X-ray. Fortunately, the only damage to Hugh was a headache and a lump just below his right

Matthew Maynard meets Waqar Younis as the Pakistani arrives at Cardiff.

ear, and he was able to return to the ground. But his efforts were all in vain as, not for the first time in 1997, rain then intervened and only 90 minutes' play was possible over the final two days, with the visitors 323 runs short of avoiding an innings defeat.

The early signs were therefore very promising, both on and off the field, with Matthew Maynard forming an effective partnership with new coach Duncan Fletcher. The former Zimbabwean captain had a fine coaching record with Western Province, and had been the coach of the South African A side on their tour to England in 1996. Warwickshire also expressed an interest in Fletcher's services as a replacement for Bob Woolmer, but Glamorgan got in first with an offer to the quiet Zimbabwean and secured his services.

As well as his shrewd advice and tactical nous, 'Fletch' became a shoulder on which Maynard could lean, and as the pressure mounted during 1997, there was no repetition of the volatile outburst Matthew Maynard had made following Glamorgan's dramatic defeat in the Benson & Hedges semi-finals the previous year, that had ended up with the Glamorgan captain receiving a rap over the knuckles and a hefty fine after publically criticising an umpire.

Glamorgan's new management team were able to toast their first Championship success of 1997 as Glamorgan defeated Kent at Canterbury, with spinners Robert Croft and Dean Cosker taking 12 wickets in the match. At the end of May, Glamorgan moved to the top of the Championship table with an innings victory over Durham, with their success following a huge first innings total of 597 for 8, the club's highest in first-class cricket. The carnage began with Steve James hitting a century before lunch and sharing an opening stand of 229 with Hugh Morris, who also made a hundred. Matthew Maynard then applied the *coup de grâce* with the third century of the innings to see the side to their record total.

The Welsh county were then brought back down to earth with a jolt as they lost to Oxford University – their first defeat to the students since 1930, albeit with a young and inexperienced side, but not before Mike Powell, a twenty-year-old batsman from Abergavenny, had scored a double hundred on his first-class debut.

MJP – I'd had a good run in the seconds, but I had never opened before that game at Oxford. Even though it was against a university side, it was still my County debut, and I was a bit anxious beforehand. But things went well early on, although on Teletext it came up that I was out, and my family didn't know for a while how well I was actually doing.

I was still not out at lunch so Darren Thomas said to me 'you could get a hundred on debut if you carry on.' I did just that and kept going too, before later in the afternoon, acting captain Tony Cottey told me that we had an hour or so before he was going to declare, and that I should try and get 200 before then. Gary Butcher was going well at the other end, and this helped to take the pressure off me. I eventually reached 200, Cotts declared and I felt very proud walking off with a double hundred to my name.

A few weeks later I made my Championship debut against Worcestershire, and I was brought back down to earth with a duck in the first innings. Even so, it was a brilliant feeling to find myself in the Glamorgan dressing room, surrounded by so many fine players. I couldn't actually believe that I was playing alongside Waqar. I never thought I would ever play in the same team as him – it was amazing to watch him running in hard every day. He always gave 100 per cent and he was a great inspiration – someone you just had to look up to.

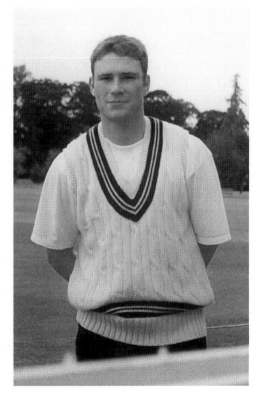

After their defeat against Oxford University, Glamorgan returned to Championship action against Middlesex at Cardiff. It turned out to be an unusual

Mike Powell – on his debut at Oxford in 1997.

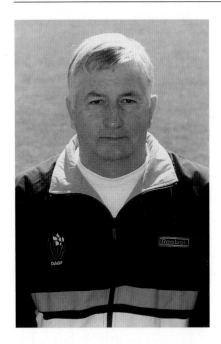

Duncan Fletcher.
Opposite: Hugh Morris batting at Swansea.

game in many ways, especially as Glamorgan's batting disintegrated after lunch on the third day as they were bowled out for 31 – the fourth lowest total in Glamorgan's history – with Jamie Hewitt taking a career-best 6-14.

MPM – *It was a bit of a freak and one of those things that happens once in a blue moon. Every ball that kept low was straight and got an lbw and every good ball got a nick and went to a hand. It was embarrassing to be rolled over for 31, but there was nothing we could have done to prevent it. There were a couple of players with their heads down afterwards. But I said to them they could walk out of the ground with their heads held high. You don't become a bad side overnight, and there are unexplained things that just happen in cricket. That was one of them.*

Matthew Maynard.

Glamorgan swiftly put these disappointments behind them on the first day of their next Championship match at Liverpool. Their batsmen had made quite serene progress to 173-1, with Steve James unbeaten on 99, when rain forced the teams from the field; no more play was possible until the morning session on the final day, so James remained marooned one short of his hundred for three days. He eventually got there on the Saturday morning, before some declaration bowling allowed Glamorgan to set Lancashire a target of 273 from 60 overs. Then in the space of just 14 overs, Waqar and 'Watty' blew their resistance away, dismissing Lancashire for 51 with Waqar taking 7-25, including a hat-trick – the first by a Glamorgan bowler in the Championship for 29 years.

After his remarkable spell, Waqar was very modest about his achievements. 'It really came together bowling from the Mersey End at Liverpool. I might have got seven, but Steve Watkin bowled really well too. I didn't know I was on a hat-trick, and I didn't

Waqar Younis and young Glamorgan fans at Cardiff in 1997.

Adrian Dale hits a four.

realise these were my career-best figures. But it's really nice to do it for Glamorgan, especially as I had not had the best of starts. I had a cracked bone in my foot when I arrived. I knew it wasn't really bad, but an injury is an injury and I wasn't really fit enough at the start. The weather also didn't help – it was really cold and it just seemed to be raining all the time. But I've got it together now, and I've found my rhythm.'

MPM – *Waqar was in awesome form with the ball and that was the most destructive spell of bowling I have seen at first-class level. I feel that this game at Liverpool was the defining moment of the season because after it all the players knew we were genuine title contenders.*

Darren Thomas – one of the young bowlers to benefit from Waqar's presence on the field, and his shrewd advice.

Adrian Shaw in action behind the stumps against Lancashire.

If anyone had any lingering doubts about Glamorgan's title aspirations, they were quickly erased in the following home game, against Sussex at Swansea. On a damp pitch and in moist air, Glamorgan struggled at first, scoring 172, but then Sussex crumbled for 54 as Waqar took 8 for 17.

James and Maynard then shared a partnership of 119 for the third wicket, and became the only two batsmen to reach double figures as the Sussex bowlers exploited the lively wicket. Set 302 to win, it was the turn of Darren Thomas and Robert Croft to then wreak havoc in Sussex's ranks as the visitors subsided again for 67 – the third successive innings against Glamorgan that was under a hundred – with Thomas taking 5-24 and Croft 3-9 from eight overs.

At the start of July, they maintained their Championship momentum with a 10-wicket victory over Gloucestershire and enjoyed a good run in the NatWest Trophy. Up to that point, it had been quite a disappointing season in the one-day games. They failed to qualify for the final stages of the Benson & Hedges competition, and Maynard's team continued to perform erratically in the Sunday League. But they enjoyed much more success in the NatWest, beating Bedfordshire by seven wickets, and then defeating Hampshire by two wickets in a game that ebbed and flowed all day on an excellent batting wicket at Southampton.

After being put in, Hampshire made 302-6 with Robin Smith scoring a forthright century. Chasing this sizeable target, Glamorgan needed a good start, but pinch-hitter Robert Croft was out in the first over, before Hugh Morris and Adrian Dale shared a century partnership for the second wicket, and the game was finely balanced at tea with Glamorgan on 113-0 after 25 overs. Their progress was halted as they lost Dale, Morris and Cottey in the space of six overs after the interval, and Steve James was then joined by Matthew Maynard. However, when the captain was dismissed, a further 111 was required from the final 16 overs, and as Adrian Shaw made his way to the wicket, Hampshire seemed to be in the box seat.

ADS – *I hadn't had my best-ever day earlier behind the stumps, but when I went out to bat, I was still thinking in a positive way. It was a bit of a pressure situation, but the wicket was a*

Steve James lets John Stephenson knows what he thinks after the Hampshire captain attempted to run out Adrian Shaw.

Robert Croft.

good one, and our best chance of winning was for me to hang on in there with Steve, push plenty of singles and give him as much of the strike as possible.

Shaw and James duly launched a spirited counter-attack, which also included a moment of controversy as Shaw appeared to be run out as Udal gathered a throw from Matthew Hayden with the Glamorgan wicketkeeper out of his ground. The umpire raised his finger, and the doughty wicketkeeper started to walk off, but Udal was unsure whether or not he had the ball in his grasp as he broke the stumps. Some of the Hampshire players suggested that Shaw should be recalled, and Steve James vented his feelings with a face-to-face conversation with Hampshire captain, John Stephenson.

MPM – Steve saw that Udal had not broken the stumps with the ball, and that's why he got a bit aggressive. Adrian was obviously concerned about the situation, but being a youngster, if a guy says you are out, you think you ought to walk. Luckily, Steve was at the other end – an old head who was not afraid to question the decision.

ADS – I walked off really slowly to give them the chance to call me back. I felt that the slower I walked back, the more chance I had!

Udal himself felt that good sportsmanship should prevail, and the two umpires recalled Shaw as the appeal was withdrawn. The two Glamorgan batsmen then continued the fight-back, until, with 11 runs needed, James was caught behind off Cardigan Connor. Darren Thomas was quickly dismissed as the tension mounted, but Waqar Younis then strode in to help Shaw take Glamorgan to a two-wicket victory. By this time, Adrian Shaw had cemented a regular place in both Glamorgan's one-day and Championship side, as Matthew Maynard opted for Shaw's run-scoring abilities rather than Metson's craft as a 'keeper. But Waqar's recruitment in place of Ottis Gibson had weakened Glamorgan's lower-middle order, and as Shaw proved at Southampton, his batting was invaluable.

ADS – *When Waqar made the winning hit, I felt a feeling of total elation – it was great to be out there and to have played a role in the victory. Taking over from Colin Metson*

Robert Croft being made a member of the Gorsedd at the 1997 Eisteddfod.

Waqar Younis.   Tony Cottey

behind the stumps, was very much like the Wales outside-half syndrome – you will always be under the microscope, but that pressure is what makes you perform as a sportsman.

The reward for the nail-biting victory over Hampshire was a home quarter-final tie against Yorkshire, and after all of the tension at Southampton, Glamorgan's fans believed that the match with the Tykes could surely not be as exciting. But how wrong they were. The match at Cardiff proved to be another cliff-hanger as Glamorgan, chasing a target of 237, had a mid-innings wobble, and lost 7 wickets for 69 runs, including captain Maynard who was suffering from chickenpox.

When last man Dean Cosker, the nineteen-year-old spin bowler, joined Waqar Younis at the crease, 28 runs were still needed. Waqar then had a moment of good fortune, surviving a sharp chance to Michael Vaughan, and then, drawing on all of his international experience, the Pakistani farmed the strike against Darren Gough and Craig White, with Cosker showing great maturity, well beyond his years, to take Glamorgan to a thrilling and remarkable one-wicket win.

DAC – *This was one of my first big one-day County games. The atmosphere and the crowd were great and I just thrived on the adrenalin out there. I took three wickets when the Yorkies batted – one of these was Martyn Moxon and getting him out gave me great confidence which I was to need later in the day batting with Waqar. I didn't feel too nervous because when you are out there you just rely on your instincts.*

Waqar was so cool under pressure. He kept talking to me all the time – his words to me were keep taking the run rate down, watch the ball and don't get out. Coming from one of the legends of the game, you try and listen. I survived a shout for lbw off Gough as the ball started reversing a great deal, but when Chris Silverwood bowled a wide, we had won a quite remarkable game!

Essex were Glamorgan's opponents for the semi-final, and the encounter at Chelmsford, like the games at Cardiff and Southampton, also contained much tension and a few sparks of controversy. The game began with Essex opting to field first, and after the loss of an hour's play, Steve James anchored the Glamorgan innings with a fine century. His team were quite satisfied to reach 301-8 in their 60 overs, but Essex quickly raced to 157-1 at tea, and with Stuart Law in imperious form, it looked as if Essex would romp to a comfortable victory.

But Steve Watkin then dismissed Darren Robinson and Nasser Hussain, before Ronnie Irani and Paul Grayson steadied the ship with the Essex score on 280 for 4 – it looked as if Glamorgan's dreams of a Lord's final were over for another year. However, Darren Thomas then turned the game around with 4-14 from 19 balls as Essex's batting disintegrated in the fading light and Glamorgan dramatically came back into the match. Maynard then called Waqar back into the attack with Essex still needing six runs with two wickets in hand and 42 balls remaining. But by now it was 8.10 p.m. and the light was very gloomy, and after just one ball from the Pakistani, the umpires consulted and took the players off the field.

MPM – *It was getting quite dark out there. Everyone would have liked to have seen a result, but it was not to be that evening. I didn't blame the batsmen out there for wanting to come off because we were on a roll. If Glamorgan had been in their position, I would have left it up to the batsmen out there to decide and, as it turned out, Ilott made the right decision.*

After another interruption on the reserve day, Waqar duly completed his over for the addition of a further three runs. Thomas then struck again with his first delivery, and as Peter Such, the number 11, strode to the wicket, Glamorgan were favourites again.

SDT – *Peter Such had a bit of a reputation of being a walking wicket, but this wasn't to be. I tried to set him up firstly with a few short balls that he fended off from his nose. Then I bowled a couple of yorkers – both of which narrowly missed his leg stump. I then tried to hit the base of his off stump, but it wasn't to be. I must have overcompensated and ended up bowling a juicy full toss which he hit with the middle of his bat and the ball sped to the boundary to win Essex the game. This match was the most frustrating so far in my career. To amass 300 in a one-day game and still lose was gutting to say the least, especially as we had fought back so well.*

The titanic battle with Essex will also be remembered as the game that saw Robert Croft hit the headlines on the 'News at Ten' after a much overblown incident with

Mark Ilott as the contest boiled up into a tense finish on the first night. As the light deteriorated, Essex had opted to stay on the field, but then as it became dimmer and Glamorgan claimed a few wickets, Essex wanted to come off. Whatever the rights and wrongs of this incident, it showed the deep passions and desire to win in both teams, and that Croft, perhaps, was more sinned against than sinning as he and Ilott had a frank exchange of views, plus a little bit of pushing, before the umpires took the players off the field. Remarkably, their altercation, replayed countless times on television, sent newspaper columnists into a frenzy of activity, claiming that cricket in modern Britain had reached a dreadful state. The two counties, quite rightly, fined the two players, but then the ECB decided that the weight of media hype also prompted a response, described by some as an over-reaction, by putting both Ilott and Croft on probation.

It had been quite a hectic few weeks for Croft, what with Glamorgan's success in the Championship, inclusion in England's Ashes squad, and being made a member of the Gorsedd in a ceremony at the Eisteddfod at Bala – hence the Gren cartoon below from the *South Wales Echo*, and the cartoonist's whimsical view about the incident at Chelmsford. Perhaps the greatest irony was that the two players were the best of friends, and when Essex played at Cardiff later in the season, the two players and their wives went out for a meal.

As Ilott said later, 'Robert and I are very good friends, have been for years and will be for years. What happened was just two people up for a game of cricket. It was not

"Its origins are losts in the mists of time – something to do with the traditional punishment for anyone who thumps a druid."

What Gren of the *South Wales Echo* thought of the Chelmsford incident!

anything more than a few frayed tempers. If it had happened in the school playground, nothing at all would have been said. Unfortunately, it was on television in front of millions. Even so, it was hardly the heavyweight championship of the world – more like Spice Boy against Spice Girl, and I'm not saying who was who!'

The one-wicket defeat at Chelmsford meant that as the players returned to Championship action, they knew their only chance of silverware lay in the four-day games. But they slid to third in the table after losing at Worcester, and all this after Matthew Maynard had played what Tom Graveney had described as the finest innings he had ever seen on the New Road ground. Although Steve James struck his fifth century of the summer, none of the Glamorgan batsmen could master an accurate Worcestershire attack chasing 374 to win from 81 overs.

However, Glamorgan returned to the top of the Championship table at the end of August after a six-wicket victory over Northamptonshire at Abergavenny. Their win was based on a pair of centuries from the prolific Steve James, and his fine batting helped to overcome the loss of Hugh Morris, who twisted an ankle in the warm-up before the start of play, and the absence of Matthew Maynard in the second innings after the Glamorgan skipper dislocated a finger. Waqar also played a role by picking up ten wickets on the lifeless Avenue Road wicket.

With four games remaining and both Surrey and Kent in the title hunt, every match and every bonus point became vital as the Welsh county maintained their Championship quest. But rain interfered with Glamorgan's match at Leicester and with Surrey also breathing down their throats, Glamorgan's contest at The Oval assumed extra significance. After securing a first innings lead of 234, and with Surrey on 32 for 3 in their second innings, it looked as if Glamorgan might wrap up a victory inside three days. But Graham Thorpe fought back with a classy double hundred, and in dubious light, Glamorgan called off their chase of 254 in 46 overs in the final session, knowing that the draw extinguished Surrey's hopes of a title challenge.

Welsh joy at the ending of Surrey's title quest was short-lived as news came through that Kent had defeated Gloucestershire to leap-frog 12 points clear at the top of the table. Glamorgan knew they now had to secure maximum points and a win over Essex in the next game at Cardiff. They secured full batting points by making 361 and then forced Essex to follow on. The visitors applied themselves better in the second innings, and Ronnie Irani and Paul Grayson staged something of a fightback.

SPJ – *Waqar had been signed to take wickets at important times, and when we needed him to step up a gear, he always did the business. As Essex recovered, Irani tried to wind up Waqar by hitting him straight back over his head on a couple of occasions. This was something that Waqar really hated and after one blow by Irani back over Waqar's head, Grayson went down the wicket and said to Irani 'I don't think you should have done that.' He was proved right as Waqar really stormed in and clean bowled Irani, sending him on his way by saying 'It was a shame you couldn't hit that one' – or words to that effect!*

Steve Watkin was also in fine form again with ball, taking 5 for 68 to leave Glamorgan with a target of 149 to win, but the nerve ends were jangling in the Glamorgan dressing room as Maynard's team slumped to 26 for 3.

PAC – *It was a low, dry wicket and the ball was starting to turn for Peter Such. We had a bit of luck that day though, as Matthew survived a chance early on behind the wicket. I was just getting into form having had quite a modest year. I knew I had to bat for as long as possible and tried to put the score out of my mind.*

MPM – *Smaller targets are often harder to reach than larger ones. It's all in the mind and you tend to think small, batting with caution instead of getting on with it. Tony Cottey joined me at the wicket and we somehow managed to survive until lunch, playing and missing and looking unsure of ourselves. 'Fletch' had a word with us during the break and told us to play normally, and not worry about the circumstances. Cotts started to go down the wicket to Such and used all of his experience to nullify the spin. Within an hour, we had won by seven wickets.*

Kent could only manage a draw with Yorkshire so Glamorgan travelled to Taunton one point above Kent and knowing that they needed to beat Somerset and pick up full points to bring the Championship pennant back to Wales for the first time since 1969. But their plans were hit soon after arriving in Taunton, when Waqar was struck down with a throat infection. Despite a high temperature, he ventured onto the field and played a role as Somerset were dismissed for 252.

Glamorgan ended the first day on 159-2, but their hopes of building up a sizeable lead were hit on the second day as rain set in, and prevented play from starting until 4 p.m. It was still quite overcast as Hugh Morris and Matthew Maynard walked out to bat, but for the next couple of hours the two batsmen produced a vintage display of batsmanship, adding 235 in 41 overs. Maynard, in particular, was in ruthless and commanding form, scoring a memorable hundred achieved without a single and all with four lights shining on the scoreboard.

MPM – *As we walked out to bat on the second afternoon, I thought to myself well, the wicket isn't going to get any worse for a while, and if we play well and bat positively, it was our best chance of quickly getting on top and putting Somerset under pressure.*

SPJ – *That was the best innings I've ever seen from Matthew. The ball was swinging around in the overcast conditions, and both Andy Caddick and Graham Rose were bowling huge away-swingers. But Matthew just kept whacking the ball through mid-on.*

Hugh Morris took his score to 165 the next day, and after some lusty blows from Robert Croft and Adrian Shaw, Glamorgan secured a 275-run lead. When Somerset batted again, Waqar was flayed to all parts of the Taunton ground, conceding 38 runs in three wayward overs, and as news filtered through about Kent's healthy progress against Surrey, it looked as if Glamorgan might be pipped at the post.

Steve James and Hugh Morris walk out from the Taunton dressing rooms to start Glamorgan's second innings.

Andy Caddick bowling in Somerset's match at Cardiff, watched by Hugh Morris and umpire Barry Dudleston.

ADS – I was worried that we had come so close, yet were still so far away. In the dressing room, I'd been watching the Teletext scores from the Surrey v. Kent match and as the Somerset batsmen settled in, I couldn't help thinking that all it needed was for them to play out the day, for the rain to come and wash out the final day at Taunton and for Kent to go on and win at Canterbury and snatch the title!

But Darren Thomas then delivered one of the most important spells of his career and together with Steve Watkin reduced Somerset to 166-7, with Thomas dismissing Mark Lathwell and Rob Turner with a couple of superb deliveries. Graham Rose and Andy Caddick then mounted a rearguard action, and the pair had added 95 before Rose was adjudged caught behind off Watkin, who also dismissed Kevin Shine for a duck, and then Dean Cosker wrapped up the innings by having Ben Trott leg before.

It meant Glamorgan needed 11 runs to win, and as Steve James and Hugh Morris walked out to the wicket, some of the Welsh voices in the crowd started the celebrations. These seemed a little premature, as Caddick raced in to bowl at James and the prolific opener, for once in 1997, had difficulty in laying a bat on the England bowler. The two had crossed swords on several occasions in the past, and Caddick was not one to miss an opportunity in letting Steve know what he thought of him. Caddick's mood became darker, and his oaths even louder, as a couple of appeals were turned down by the umpires.

SPJ – *I will not forget that innings at Taunton as long as I live. The prospect of needing to score just 11 got to me more than any other innings I have played. It was the most nervous I have ever been on a cricket field. I didn't really want to bat and I had hoped we wouldn't need to. Caddick was at the top of the Whyte and Mackay Rankings at the time, and as there was a bit of money in it, he was keen to get a few more scalps.*

HM – *I was hoping the joke bowlers would come on, and I wasn't too pleased to see Andy Caddick roaring in to bowl in that light. But we were only out there for eight balls, and when Steve hit that ball to the long-leg boundary for four, my only thought was to grab those three stumps and get off the pitch quickly.*

SPJ – *When I actually hit the ball, I thought we would get one run, maybe two if I ran quickly. But when I got down the other end and turned around I saw Hugh picking up the stumps and running off. I still thought we needed one more to win, and quickly realised that I had miscounted.*

For a few seconds, Steve must have been the only person in the ground not to realise what had happened as the ball sped to the boundary boards and it was not long before the Taunton outfield was covered in happy Welshman as the players and their loyal

Hugh Morris races off from the Taunton ground after the winning runs had been hit.

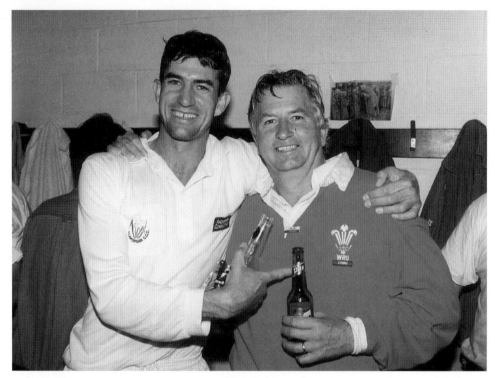

Steve Watkin (left) and Duncan Fletcher (right) in the Taunton dressing room.

band of supporters celebrated the club's first Championship success since 1969. The champagne corks were soon flying out from the visitors balcony whilst below, the songs began, with chants of 'Waqar is a Welshman' reverberating around the County Ground. News came through that Kent had beaten Surrey, but it didn't matter a jot – Glamorgan were the County Champions of 1997.

SLW – *For me as an individual, playing for England was the highlight of my career, but from a team point of view, and as a proud Welshman, this betters it all. When everyone starts off playing county cricket, they want to win the County Championship. I made my debut in 1986 so I waited eleven years for those moments at Taunton, and to finally do it was a fantastic feeling. Whoever wins the Championship is generally the best side in the country. We played sixteen games that summer and dominated thirteen of them. But for the weather I think we would have already won the title before the game with Somerset, and would have gone down to Taunton for four days of fun!*

PAC – *As soon as we won the game, I went over to Watty. We started together as seventeen year olds in the Second XI when we were the whipping boys of the circuit. But a good hard bunch of cricketers came through and we turned it around from being a losing side. At the end of the day, we were definitely the best side of 1997.*

MPM – *It was such a big thing for us all. We never lost faith, we never lost heart and we did it. It was a real pleasure to lead the team. Privately, I felt that we could win the title right from the first game of the season against Warwickshire. We annihilated them over two days and the way we performed in that game set the tone for the summer. It was a very hard season, but a very enjoyable one. What pleased me was that we coped with the pressure as it increased. In our biggest game of the season we won by ten wickets. We had to get 24 points to be sure of winning the title and we did it in two days and a session – what more can you say.*

RDBC – *We came in for a bit of stick in certain quarters about not being the best team in the Championship. But people who say things in haste in the papers often live to regret it. We did our talking on the field and proved our worth. In many ways, 1997 was a difficult year for me, but it turned out to be one of the best years of my life. I had grown up with the lads in the Glamorgan team, and we had seen some bad times together. In 1997 we gave something back to each other, and that day at Taunton was one that I will savour for the rest of my life. In rugby terms, our success in the Sunday League in 1993 was like winning a seven-a-side tournament. Winning the County Championship was like lifting the European Cup in rugby or the Premiership in soccer.*

SDT – *It seemed the whole of Wales was watching and the noise was deafening. The atmosphere was so good, it was as if we were playing at home. It was incredible to*

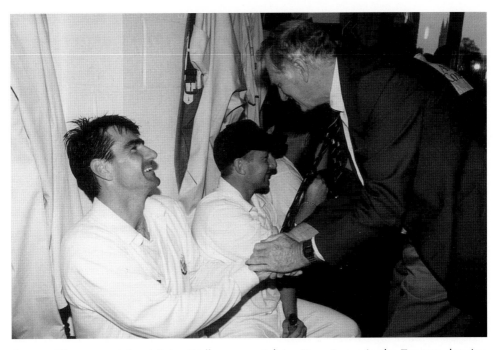

Former Glamorgan stalwart Peter Walker congratulates Steve James in the Taunton dressing room.

The Glamorgan team on their open top bus ride through Cardiff after becoming the County Champions of 1997.

be out in the middle as the story unfolded – the ball was moving about and I managed to get it going away from the left-handers and they had three in their top five. Before we went out for the second innings, Hugh Morris told me that he thought it would be my day. I had bowled quite well in the first innings, without much luck, but this time the edges were found. I will never forget the celebrations and I was lost for words for a while as our achievements about becoming County Champions started to sink in.

But not all of the Glamorgan squad were able to make it to Taunton to join in with the celebrations. One of these was Gary Butcher.

GB – I had planned to travel down for the final day at Taunton, but when the wickets started to tumble on the Saturday afternoon, I decided to try to get to Taunton. I had Darren Thomas' car, but he didn't tell me that he had an immobiliser on it. I couldn't start it and I had to go back into the house and watch the end of the game on televi-

sion. It felt strange sitting there on my own watching the lads win the Championship, but I was really thrilled about it.

After the winning runs had been hit, Steve James had stopped to uproot the stumps and grab a souvenir, but he ended up in a mêlée of ecstatic Glamorgan fans, one of whom grabbed Steve's bat from his grasp and ran off with it.

SPJ – *I was quite upset to lose the bat, because it meant a lot to me, and had brought me a lot of runs. The fact that it hit the runs that brought us the Championship made it even more special to me, so I appealed to a local newspaper to have it returned. Fortunately, it came back just before we started our official celebrations back in Cardiff.*

The celebrations at Sophia Gardens and on an open top bus tour around the Welsh capital were also given extra meaning following confirmation that Hugh Morris would be retiring at the end of the season to take over the post of the ECB's Technical Director.

HM – *I had mixed emotions following my appointment. Having just helped Glamorgan to win the Championship for the first time since 1969, it was a huge wrench for me to leave the County. But it is always easier to go out on a high, and there could be no bigger high than winning the Championship. I still feel very proud to have played my part in achieving this success for Welsh cricket.*

Robert Croft, Matthew Maynard and Steve James with the Championship Trophy.

Matthew Maynard – a proud Glamorgan captain.

A scriptwriter could have hardly penned a more fitting finale in Glamorgan's ranks than the one Hugh Morris enjoyed at Taunton, with the thirty-four year old signing off with the 52nd century of his career, to equal the club record held by Alan Jones, and in front of several of his mentors from Blundell's School in Devon, where he had created so many records as a schoolboy batsman.

HM – *I was really proud of this final century, especially as it came in such an important game, and I was pleased how I performed under the pressure and up against such a good attack. I knew it might be my final game, and I knew I was one short of equalling Alan Jones' record. Throughout my career, I had always set myself goals and targets, so it was fantastic to finish level with Alan, and to do so in the game when Glamorgan became Champions.*

It was also poignant that the title was secured in the year that Wilf Wooller, the club's *eminance grise*, had passed away. Wilf had been the spiritual backbone of the club since the Second World War, and the previous summer had even popped into the Glamorgan dressing room with a few words of advice on field placing and tactics. No doubt, the great skipper was looking down on Taunton from on high, demanding a few fielding or bowling changes, before, in typical Wooller fashion, joining in with the heady celebrations that went on long into the night at Taunton to celebrate what had become the Year of the Daffodil.

Glamorgan in the County Championship - 1997

23-26 April at Sophia Gardens, Cardiff
Warwickshire 151 (S.L. Watkin 3-32, S.D. Thomas 4-62) and 77-3
Glamorgan 551-3 dec (H. Morris 233, A. Dale 106, S.P. James 83)
Match Drawn

7-10 May at Headingley
Glamorgan 336(S.P. James 109, H. Morris 55, R.D.B. Croft 57) and 166-2 dec
   (H. Morris 96, S.P. James 52)
Yorkshire 200 (D.S. Lehmann 54, R.D.B. Croft 4-58)
Match Drawn

14-17 May at Canterbury
Glamorgan 279 (M.J. McCague 6-75) and 193 (S.P. James 54, P.A. Strang 4-59,
   M.V. Fleming 4-28)
Kent 154 (S.D. Thomas 3-13, R.D.B. Croft 5-33) and 231 (A.P. Wells 85, D.A. Cosker 4-64)
Glamorgan won by 87 runs

21-24 May at Sophia Gardens, Cardiff
Hampshire 309-4 (R.A. Smith 94, K.D. James 85) and forfeited second inns
Glamorgan forfeited first inns and 287-8 (S.P. James 76, G.P. Butcher 58)
Match Drawn

29 May - 2 June at Sophia Gardens, Cardiff
Glamorgan 597-8 dec (S.P. James 153, H. Morris 135, M.P. Maynard 134)
Durham 345 (M.J. Foster 129, S.L. Watkin 4-73) and 244 (J.E. Morris 149,
   Waqar Younis 4-56)
Glamorgan won by an innings and 8 runs

12-14 June at Sophia Gardens, Cardiff
Glamorgan 281 (R.D.B. Croft 82, M.P. Maynard 59, A.R.C. Fraser 4-68) and 31
   (J.P. Hewitt 6-14, A.R.C. Fraser 4-17)
Middlesex 319 (J.H. Kallis 96, S.L. Watkin 4-43, S.D. Thomas 4-52)
Middlesex won by an innings and 7 runs

18-21 June at Liverpool
Glamorgan 272-1 dec (S.P. James 152*, A. Dale 78*) and forfeited second inns
Lancashire forfeited first inns and 51 (Waqar Younis 7-25, S.L. Watkin 3-21)
Glamorgan won by 221 runs

26-30 June at Swansea
Glamorgan 172 (S.P. James 48, R.J. Kirtley 6-60) and 183-9 dec
    (S.P. James 82*, M.P. Maynard 61, M.A. Robinson 4-41)
Sussex 54 (Waqar Younis 8-17) and 67 (S.D. Thomas 5-24, R.D.B. Croft 3-9)
Glamorgan won by 234 runs

2-5 July at Swansea
Glamorgan 400-5 dec (H. Morris 173, M.P. Maynard 98, P.A. Cottey 76*) and 52-0
Gloucestershire 214 (Waqar Younis 3-55, S.L. Watkin 3-61, D.A. Cosker 3-59)
    and 233 (M.W. Alleyne 42, S.D. Thomas 3-40, D.A. Cosker 4-87)
Glamorgan won by 10 wickets

23-26 July at Chesterfield
Derbyshire 513-6 dec (A.S. Rollins 148, M.R. May 116) and 35-0
Glamorgan 364 (A. Dale 142, P.A.J. DeFreitas 3-86)
Match Drawn

31 Jul-4 August at Colwyn Bay
Nottinghamshire 202 (M.P. Dowman 62, R.D.B. Croft 3-46, Waqar Younis 3-66)
    and 239 (C.M. Tolley 73*, R.D.B. Croft 3-52)
Glamorgan 353-6 dec (S.P. James 162)
Match Drawn

15-18 August at Worcester
Worcestershire 476-9 dec (T.S. Curtis 160, G.A. Hick 65, G.P. Butcher 3-87, R.D.B. Croft
    3-80) and 295 (W.P.C. Weston 114, Waqar Younis 3-50, R.D.B. Croft 4-98)
Glamorgan 398 (M.P. Maynard 161*, S.P. James 69, G.R. Haynes 3-46) and 319
    (S.P. James 130, M.M. Mirza 3-53)
Worcestershire won by 54 runs

20-23 August at Abergavenny
Northamptonshire 330 (K.M. Curran 159, Waqar Younis 4-78, R.D.B. Croft 3-68)
    and 219 (D.J.G. Sales 103, Waqar Younis 6-56)
Glamorgan 354-6 dec (S.P. James 103, A. Dale 71, M.P. Maynard 58) and 197-4
    (S.P. James 113)
Glamorgan won by 6 wickets

27-30 August at Leicester
Glamorgan 226 (A. Dale 69, D.J. Millns 3-58, D. Williamson 3-19) and 67-3
Leicestershire 175 (J.J. Whitaker 62, S.L. Watkin 7-41)
Match drawn

2-5 September at The Oval
Surrey 204 (A.D. Brown 60, S.D. Thomas 3-36, R.D.B. Croft 3-54) and 487
    (G.P. Thorpe 222, D.A. Cosker 3-107)

Glamorgan 438 (A. Dale 72, M.P. Maynard 76, S.D. Thomas 75*, R.D.B. Croft 53)
   and 107-3
Match Drawn

10-13 September at Sophia Gardens, Cardiff
Glamorgan 361 (H. Morris 82, M.P. Maynard 71, D.R. Law 4-69) and 150-3
   (M.P. Maynard 75*)
Essex 169 (S.G. Law 85, Waqar Younis 3-31, S.L. Watkin 3-68) and 340
   (A.P. Grayson 98, S.L. Watkin 5-68)
Glamorgan won by 7 wickets

18-20 September at Taunton
Somerset 252 (P.D. Bowler 63, Waqar Younis 4-41, S.L. Watkin 3-61) and 285
   (G.D. Rose 67, A.R. Caddick 56, S.D. Thomas 5-38)
Glamorgan 527 (H. Morris 165, M.P. Maynard 142, R.D.B. Croft 86, A.D. Shaw 53)
   and 11-0
Glamorgan won by 10 wickets

9

'Fletch'

As the Glamorgan team went on an open-top bus tour of Cardiff, Waqar Younis paid handsome tribute to the rest of the side, as well as the club's loyal supporters for all that they had done in 1997.

WY – Living and playing in Wales is quite unlike anything I experienced in three years at The Oval. London is a huge, cosmopolitan city, where it is easy to be anonymous. Nobody much cares that you are a leading cricketer; they have other much more important matters on their mind. But wherever I have been with Glamorgan, it is as if they have all known me forever. Complete strangers have come up to me and wanted to shake my hand simply because I came to play here. It is almost like living in a village where everybody knows everybody else, and it makes me very aware of their aspirations.

The bowler also said that he had turned down an SOS call from an injury-hit Pakistan side who wanted Waqar to join them in a one-day tournament in Canada. However, Waqar was not going to desert his Welsh colleagues in their hour of need.

WY – The Pakistani Board asked me to go out to Canada to cover for players who were injured. But I told had them earlier in the year that if Glamorgan had any chance of winning the Championship I would be staying in Wales. I love to play for my country, but something historic was going to happen here and I wanted to be part of it.

Waqar's presence on the field, as well as his bowling partnership with Steve Watkin, were two major factors in Glamorgan's success.

SIW – Waqar was exactly what we needed – a player who had a huge psychological effect on our opponents. He did not even have to be bowling to have them thinking about what might happen when he came on, and any relief opponents had when he finished a spell was tempered by the knowledge that he would be coming back at some stage. Waqar and I also made a natural pair of opening bowlers. He is a strike bowler, always trying to take wickets. Consistency was always my strength, and it may have been that batsmen, happy to be away from Waqar, tried to have a go at me instead!

SDT – Waqar took the burden of the attack off Watty's very heavy shoulders and led from the front with a string of match-winning performances. He gave the side a lot of self belief and was also quite a character in the changing room – this was awesome

Duncan Fletcher flanked on the Cardiff balcony by a smiling Matthew Maynard and a pensive Dean Cosker.

for team spirit. He also did wonders for me. He always put the opposition batsmen under pressure and that meant I was able to come on feeling a lot more relaxed. When I came on for Waqar, batsmen were looking to throw the bat at me a bit and get a few runs on the board before Robert Croft came on and tied them up. That was fine by me because it meant they were going to get nicks and that meant I was going to get wickets. I also got an opportunity to bowl early on with Waqar bowling shorter spells, and I got a choice of ends at first change. The previous seasons I had been bowling into the wind that made things much harder for me. When Waqar was not bowling, he stood at mid-off, focussing on the batsman to study his weaknesses. He would then come over and tell me what to be aiming for. You cannot but learn when you have a pair of opening bowlers of the calibre of Waqar Younis and Steve Watkin. I was given an immediate chance to claim the third seamer's spot and things went well for me. To take five wickets in the last innings was something else.

But Glamorgan's Championship success in 1997 was not just about the signing of Waqar Younis, and despite his haul of 68 first-class wickets, plus some entertaining little cameos with the bat, there were other important ingredients in the Welsh county's success. High on the list was the fact that Matthew Maynard could regularly call upon the same players, and in the absence of major injuries, a settled team developed.

On the batting front, all of the leading batsmen enjoyed fruitful summers, with each member complementing each other. Hugh Morris was the perfect sheet anchor, who could occupy the crease for long periods, whilst his partner, Steve James, was fleet of

Darren Thomas and Waqar Younis in the Taunton dressing room.

foot between the wickets, equally tenacious, and able to wear down opposing bowlers. James enjoyed another prolific season with 1,775 runs – nine more than the previous season. He was the first batsman in the country to score a thousand runs, and at times in 1997 it seemed that he only had to walk to the middle, and a century was his. 'Sid' deservedly won the PCA Cricketer of the Year, yet he was consistently overlooked by the England selectors, who perhaps judged him more on what he once had been, rather than what he had become. Once again, the media were surprised at James' prolific form being ignored, as the newspaper opposite shows.

Adrian Dale, the number 3, had a very adaptable style, and was able to score quickly or drop anchor, but whatever the situation, he always seemed able to almost steal runs with swift and clever singles. Matthew Maynard was the classy, imperious stroke-maker, whilst Tony Cottey was gritty and determined, ever the man for a crisis, but someone who could also press the accelerator and score quick runs if they were needed.

MPM – *I was fortunate that the people at the top of the order were in such good form that I could play five batsmen with Robert Croft coming in at 6. That meant we could play five bowlers and have a balanced attack, which is vital. I am a big believer that if five batsmen cannot get the runs, how is another batsman coming in at 6 going to get you the runs. If you play three seamers and two spinners, one of them will win the game for you.*

Maynard's imaginative captaincy and forceful leadership was another important element behind the team's success, with Maynard always being prepared to gamble if there was a chance of success. However, it was coach Duncan Fletcher who helped to gel all of these elements, and without his steady hand on the tiller, the good ship Glamorgan might not have sailed so smoothly towards the county title.

PAC – *Fletch inherited a team who were waiting to win the Championship. Waqar was the missing link that we had needed. In 1997 we had a quality quick bowler who intimidated opponents like Viv had done, and who could knock over wickets at vital times. Fletch pulled it all together, and as an outsider coming in, it meant even the established players had to prove themselves. He also brought a freshness to our approach – new ideas and new drills – so that every morning there was something different in our warm-ups.*

AD – *Fletch had a great relationship with Matthew and gave him a free rein so that he could fully express himself as a captain. Fletch was great with people, and had excellent man-management skills, whilst Matt had the character and personality as*

What the *Wales on Sunday* newspaper thought!

The Glamorgan squad celebrate on the balcony at Taunton after becoming County Champions.

a leader to make people believe in him and what he had decided.He more than led by example, playing innings nobody else could, making run outs that nobody else could and holding onto catches that nobody else could.

SLW – *Fletch gave us belief in our ability and worked us harder than ever before – not in a nasty way, but in a nice way. He had also become not used to losing when he was coaching Western Province in South Africa. Waqar was also used to success with Pakistan, so all in all, neither ever saw defeat as an option.*

'Fletch' also built on the groundwork done by John Derrick, the First XI coach in 1996, and soon developed an excellent working relationship with Matthew Maynard.

MPM – *I had sent a dossier to Fletch with notes and comments about all of the players – their character and their records. In the first week he was with us, Fletch closely watched every player and barely said a word to anyone else. Some of the boys said to me, 'Jeez, we've got a mute coach', but Fletch was just quietly observing everyone and in the second week, he started to make some shrewd suggestions and gave everyone great little tips about what to work on.*

SPJ – *His impact on the players when he first came here was astonishing. The lads were so impressed after our first meeting that it was impossible not to respect and admire him. Duncan's ability to pick up on technical faults is brilliant. He only has to watch you face or bowl two or three deliveries, and if there is something wrong, he will spot it straight away. He is also very good at relaxing people and getting us to go out and do something positive, especially a batsman who may be going through a bad time.*

MPM – 'We were totally different characters. I was outgoing and headstrong, whilst Fletch was quiet and reflective. When it came to cricket, we were on the same wavelength and he thought the coach should act as a consultant to the captain and provide a shoulder to lean on. As a coach, he is very meticulous. He does not just look at the overall picture – he tears it into a thousand pieces and studies every one. He threw ideas at us all the time which was brilliant – that is the sign of a quality coach and he brought some very good things to Glamorgan cricket.

One of these was introducing variety into our warm-up and warm-down sessions, ensuring that they were competitive exercises. By carefully dividing up the teams, these sessions allowed players to get rid of their pent-up aggression at the same time as fuelling our competitive instincts in a therapeutic sort of way. He also did not read

Duncan Fletcher and
Matthew Maynard
talking tactics at Cardiff.

Waqar Younis appealing at Cardiff.

the riot act after the 31 against Middlesex. He realised that it was a one-off, and his realistic, level-headed manner helped the team put it out of their minds, rather than making an issue of it.

MJF – *Fletch spent the first three weeks during the pre-season period getting to know Alan Jones and John Derrick. He recognised that they were men of Glamorgan, that they knew the players and domestic structure better than he did, knew the traditions, pitches, habits and characters involved. He wanted to pick their brains and by the time the first match came around, he had a clear idea of just how talented the squad was. The way the team started against Warwickshire proved to him that whilst perhaps more adept at the longer form of the game, they had the ability to challenge the very best. He ensured they never lost that self-belief.*

If one player had to be singled out as the man who derived most benefit from Fletcher's coaching, that person would be Darren Thomas. He had struggled in the previous seasons, with his bowling frequently being too wayward or erratic. The 22 year old blossomed with advice from Fletch, and stepped into Waqar Younis' shoes when the Pakistani was struck down by illness in the vital match against Somerset.

SLW – *Duncan came along at the right time, for he knew nothing of Darren's earlier career, but he instantly saw a raw, young bowler with genuine pace, even if the direction was missing. Fletch's guidance and expertise was imperative to Darren's cause and he was positive in the way he thought Darren should bowl. His confidence, allied to that of the captain, was repaid by outstanding contributions and some might say a historic performance at Taunton. During that game, I remember thinking what a good wicket it was and how both Waqar and I had taken a little stick, bowling with the new ball in Somerset's second innings. But then Darren came on to bowl a magnificent spell with both pace and movement.*

SDT – *Duncan helped me with my bowling action. I was trying to get too side-on and it was causing a lot of pain in my back. He noticed it as soon as he arrived, so I worked with him on a new run-up in the pre-season nets and developed a more front-on open-chested action like Malcolm Marshall. I think a lot of Duncan – not only he is a great coach, he is a superb bloke. As a coach, he is always searching to stay ahead of the game to invent different shots and balls especially in the one-day format. What Duncan did as well was to bring to the squad the idea that most players could not get away with just having one skill, and he made the players, especially the younger ones, work on different aspects of the game. He was also a very fine man manager – one example was including Tony Cottey in the crunch match against Essex at Cardiff. Mike Powell had been pressing for a place all season in the seconds, and breaking all kinds of records. By Cott's own admission, it wasn't one of his greatest seasons, but Duncan and Matt stuck with Cotts as they thought not only was he a good thinker of the game, but also essential to have in the changing room for team spirit in this must-win game. It turned out that Cotts played a crucial innings on a run-chase that saw us win the match.*

The 1998 season began with Glamorgan eager to consolidate on their success over the past twelve months, but the club were hit by a catalogue of injuries and could not sustain a challenge to retain the Championship title. Waqar only appeared in four Championship matches as a result of an elbow injury and he returned home very disappointed and dejected at not being able to see out his two-year contract and bring more success to Glamorgan.

Steve Watkin also broke down for the first time in his outstanding career and missed five Championship games, while the Glamorgan attack also missed Robert Croft at various times of the summer, due to England call-ups and a knee injury that necessitated an operation at the end of the summer. Darren Thomas emerged as the club's most successful bowler, taking 71 first-class wickets, and recording the club's best-ever figures in one-day cricket by taking 7-16 against Surrey in the Sunday League match at Swansea. His continued development and emerging all-round abilities were rewarded with selection for the England A tour.

SDT – *The match against Surrey was a personal highlight for me, but it only came about thanks to a superb opening spell by Owen Parkin and Steve Watkin on a very slow Swansea wicket. Then when I started bowling in the 15th over, I was fortunate that the ball was reverse-swinging, and I just tried to use the knowledge that Waqar had given me and luckily, it paid off that day.*

Another face missing in 1998 was that of Duncan Fletcher. After a continuous spell of coaching in the Cape, he had only agreed to join Glamorgan on a one-year contract for

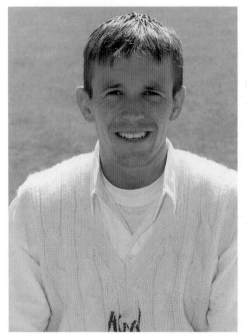

Owen Parkin.

Andrew Davies.

Ismail Dawood.

Wayne Law.

1997, but he wisely had the option of returning at a later date after a break back home in South Africa where he could recharge his batteries.

John Derrick therefore stepped back into Fletcher's shoes for 1998 and, given the catalogue of injuries and Test calls, he did very well with the resources at his disposal. 1998 saw 'J.D.' oversee Glamorgan to 4 Championship wins, 7 victories in the Sunday League as well as a remarkable success over Sri Lanka, with the World Cup Champions being dismissed on the first day for just 54 – the lowest score any Test side had ever made against Glamorgan. The tourists fared slightly better a second time around, as Adrian Dale returned match figures of 9 for 45. Despite having to face the wiles of spin bowler Muttiah Muralitharan, Glamorgan reached their target of 53 with five wickets in hand to record their first win over a touring team in first-class cricket since 1971 and their first-ever win over the Sri Lankans.

The absence of Waqar and 'Watty' gave opportunities to three younger bowlers. One of these was Owen Parkin, a twenty-five-year-old seamer, born in Coventry of Welsh parents and raised in Dorset. He had made his debut in 1994, and two years later burst into the County's one-day team with 5 for 28 against Sussex at Hove. 1998 saw 'Parky' get an opportunity with the new ball in Championship cricket, and he made the most of his opportunities. He achieved career-best figures of 5 for 24 in the final Championship match of the summer against Somerset at Cardiff as Glamorgan won by 298 runs to revive memories of the great day at Taunton twelve months before.

Andrew Davies also appeared in several games during 1998. The former Christ College, Brecon student had first played for Glamorgan in 1995, but a series of injuries had then blighted the young swing bowler's career. Now the boot was on the other foot as injuries to other bowlers gave 'Diver' a further taste of first-team cricket.

Simon Jones, the nineteen-year-old son of former England and Glamorgan pace ace, Jeff Jones, also made his first-team debut in 1998 after enjoying a successful career at Millfield School. The youngster soon had many county batsmen talking about his raw pace.

SPJo – *I'd been bowling well in the seconds, so it was great to make my county debut up at Durham. I was keen to prove myself, and everything went quite well. After the Durham innings, David Boon, their experienced Australian batsman came over and said how he had been impressed with my pace. It was a great feeling to be complimented by him.*

The batting was also handicapped by the absence for over a month of Matthew Maynard with a nasty groin injury. Overall, the captain endured a wretched season, failing to score a century in any form of cricket, and for only the second time in 13 seasons, he missed out on a thousand runs. His team also badly missed the stabilising presence, and comforting sight of Hugh Morris at the top of the order. A mix of poor form and injuries meant that there were no less than nine different opening combinations as the County experimented with a variety of different openers, including Ismail Dawood, a twenty-two-year-old batsman/wicketkeeper, who had been signed from Worcestershire over the winter months following the retirement of Colin Metson at the end of 1997.

The absence of Maynard and Morris allowed other batsmen to emerge, in particular Mike Powell, who confirmed his standing as a gifted stroke-maker. During 1998, the young batsman became a first-team regular and at Northampton he struck an impressive maiden Championship century. Wayne Law, the nineteen-year-old opening batsman from Llanelli, also hit 131 against Lancashire at Colwyn Bay, calmly striking the last two balls before lunch from Wasim Akram back over the Pakistani's head for a six and a four in a memorable and almost carefree display of batting.

There was also delight in Welsh ranks when Steve James was, at long last, called up for two Test appearances, against South Africa at Lord's.

SPJ – *It was a massive shock for me as I was a last-minute call-up for the injured Mark Butcher and had been expecting to spend my week in the relative calm of Sophia Gardens playing against Leicestershire. Suddenly I was thrust into this cauldron of noise and frenzy at the home of cricket. The heat was really turned up when it was my turn to bat on the second evening, facing an enraged Allan Donald who had been hit in the ribs by Dean Headley when batting. To make your Test debut at Lord's is what everyone dreams about. Pollock gave me a few juicy half volleys, but then Boucher took a brilliant catch and that was that. Walking out to open the batting with my old university chum, Mike Atherton, was something that I will never forget, although shuffling back through the Long Room after recording a duck in the second innings was not as enjoyable an experience.*

Despite his second innings duck, James was chosen to play against Sri Lanka at The Oval, but once again he was summoned as a late replacement and did not get the chance to properly prepare and relax with the rest of the England squad. Like Matthew Maynard before him, he also had other things on his mind, as his wife Jane was due to give birth very soon.

SPJ – *I'd woken up on the Wednesday morning thinking I would be playing in a Benefit Match for Steve Watkin up at Tondu, but then Jane started to go into labour and we went off to hospital. Then I got a phone message to ring Glamorgan, and I found out that 'Athers' was injured and that I had to report to The Oval. I stayed with Jane for a while then travelled up to London. I got a few runs on the Thursday, and after I was out, I was told that I could return to Cardiff to be with Jane. I caught the train from Paddington, and soon after eleven got back to the Heath Hospital. At 4.40 a.m. the next morning, Bethan was born and I duly caught the early morning train back up to London, hoping to get some sleep en route. But when I got onto the platform, I bumped into Ricky Needham, one of our committeemen, who was going up to London on business, so it wasn't until I got back to Lord's that I had a chance to catch up on my sleep.*

Off the field, there were other signs that the club was rapidly moving forward, especially the construction work on the National Cricket Centre, as well as preparations being set in motion for the staging of a One-Day International at Sophia Gardens, and the hosting of the Australians during the 1999 World Cup. All were signs that despite the disappointments of 1998, Glamorgan cricket was still on the up.

10

Stadium Sophia

It had always been Glamorgan's long-held dream to own a ground of their own, and a string of famous leaders from Maurice Turnbull and J.C. Clay to Wilf Wooller and Tony Lewis had harboured hopes that they might one day lead the Welsh county out onto their very own soil. Ever since their entry into first-class cricket in 1921, this had remained a pipedream with Glamorgan who at that time led a gypsy-like existence, owning just a small office complex in Cardiff city centre and playing their games at a variety of club grounds. A few schemes were hatched in the 1950s and 1960s for Glamorgan to develop their own ground, but until the 1990s all proved to be abortive.

This nomadic way of life helped the club to fly the flag, especially as Glamorgan, Wales' only first-class side, represent more than just a county borough. However, the lack of a home ground and headquarters also had its disadvantages – the costs of playing at and equipping up to eight grounds a year, the cost of renting equipment and seating, plus the lack of any winter income from bars, restaurants or conference facilities.

Things have dramatically changed in the past few years and the dreams of Turnbull and Wooller became a reality on 24 November 1995 as the club formally acquired from Cardiff Athletic Club a new 125-year lease of the Sophia Gardens ground in Cardiff, where they had been playing since 1967 following the move from their previous base at the Arms Park.

In October 1996, the club launched ambitious plans to redevelop the pretty tree-lined ground on the western banks of the Taff and create a twenty-first century head-quarters, with 24 new corporate hospitality boxes, a new media centre, an Indoor School, new practice facilities, plus new grandstands and seating enclosures, with the whole Sophia Gardens complex becoming one of the ECB's Centres of Excellence, and a base for the newly created Cricket Board of Wales.

The club secured £2.8 million of lottery funding, and the three-phase project began with work during the winter of 1998/99 on the construction of a seven-lane indoor cricket school and administration block on the site of the former scorebox at the Cathedral Road end of the ground. New seating was also erected at the river end of the ground, together with new outdoor nets, a training area and a new scoreboard facility.

HM – *This is a fantastic project that not just Glamorgan but the whole of Wales can be proud of. I'm really delighted to see the quality of the new facilities at Cardiff. It makes such a difference to have good practice facilities, both under cover and outdoors. I remember one of my first days at Glamorgan when West Indian Ezra Moseley began bowling on this artificial surface that we used to net on out in the middle of the square. Ezra was rather quick and the first ball he pitched on a length*

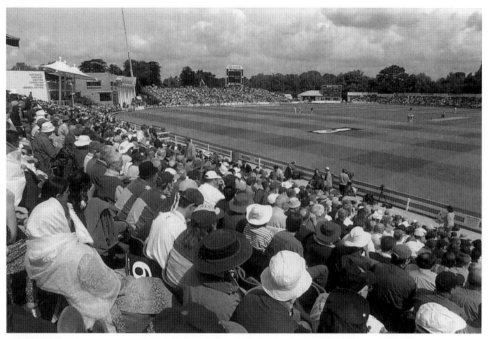

Stadium Sophia.

went past the nose of the young left-hander Mark Davies. You knew then that you were in for a tough time and that was no way to build confidence or improve technique.

SDT – *It is lovely to see the club going forward with the development of the ground. Ten years ago we wouldn't have dreamt of having an indoor cricket centre at Sophia Gardens. Pre-season used to consist of indoor nets at Neath followed by runs around The Gnoll, but now we are in and out of our eight-lane indoor nets and in the multigym.*

It's great too that gone are the days when we were in and out of portacabins to see the admin. staff. It is nice to see that they have now got good facilities and plenty of office space to work in. All in all, the development of the ground has now brought a more professional look to the club on and off the pitch and gone are the days that Glamorgan was an old-fashioned club. Three trophies in ten years, a Lord's final, and several England players coming from us, all tells a different picture. The new facilities will help the daffodil to blossom further, especially as we have something special in that we are a country playing against other counties.

The building work at Sophia Gardens was completed in time for the club to host the Australians in their preparations for the 1999 World Cup, and their match against New Zealand. There was a capacity crowd of 6,500 inside the Cardiff ground on 20 May for this Antipodean clash which saw New Zealand, the underdogs, dramatically turn the tables on the favourites for the World Cup competition. The Kiwis won by five wickets, with Geoff Allott taking four wickets and Roger Twose, the former Warwickshire batsman, smashing an unbeaten 80 to steer New Zealand to victory in a match that proved that Cardiff was a most worthy international venue, and a ground, thanks to all the hard work of Len Smith and his staff, with a top-class wicket.

Turning to the domestic front, Tony Cottey was one of the faces missing when the County's staff gathered for the photo-call in the shadow of the impressive new complex. During the winter months, the thirty-two-year-old batsman had joined Sussex, who had offered him a five-year contract, against Glamorgan's offer of two. Jacques Kallis, Glamorgan's new overseas signing, was also missing, as like other international stars, he was on World Cup duty until June.

Glamorgan had hoped that the talented all-rounder would make his County debut shortly after the end of the tournament, but the South African suffered a stomach injury and returned to the Cape for treatment, before making his long-awaited debut in July. He quickly made up for lost time with a blistering assault on the Surrey bowlers at Pontypridd, hitting an unbeaten 155 from 141 balls on his County debut. His brutal innings was the highest in the League competition and set up an emphatic 71-run victory that helped to lift the club's morale.

By the time Kallis arrived in Wales, Glamorgan had struggled in several Championship matches and had erratic form in the newly-created Second Division of the National League. Dressed in their new red and black kit, and bearing the name of the Glamorgan Dragons, the side had made a promising start in the new competition, defeating the Middlesex Crusaders and the Derbyshire Scorpions with Alun Evans scoring his maiden one-day century. But there then followed a barren patch as the

How it used to be – Wilf Wooller commentating at Cardiff as Glamorgan beat Worcestershire to become County Champions in 1969.

Hugh Morris and Matthew Maynard in front of the Indoor School at its opening in 1999.

Dragons went off the boil, and despite a late season rally, with five victories in the last seven games, the Welsh side could not mount a promotion charge, and remained in the Second Division.

The one ray of hope was in the NatWest competition. The Hampshire Board were beaten in the opening round at Southampton, before Warwickshire, Glamorgan's one-day nemesis, were defeated at Cardiff thanks to an unbeaten 118 by Steve James and an inspired bowling spell by Robert Croft, who took 3-38 before hearing that he had become a father as his wife gave birth later that night. The 6-wicket defeat of Warwickshire rewarded Glamorgan with a quarter-final tie at home to Gloucestershire, one of the most improved one-day teams in the country, and for the umpteenth time, the spectre of a Lord's final loomed on the horizon.

Inserted by Maynard on a green-looking wicket that did not misbehave, and with minimal assistance for the bowlers, Gloucestershire's openers piled on the runs, adding 142 in 30 overs. It gave the visitors the perfect launch-pad for a sizeable total, and despite a mid-innings wobble against the accurate Robert Croft, Gloucestershire finished on 274-6. Their bowlers soon made early inroads, and after sliding to 36/4, Glamorgan sank to a 136-run defeat.

MPM – *That was a very disappointing game. We did not perform as a unit and Gloucestershire gave us a lesson on how to perform in one-day cricket. Their opening bowlers put us under a lot of pressure at the start and they played well as a team.*

The end of the game was also marred by a small section of so-called supporters who hurled abuse at the Glamorgan players, swore and spat at the team's dressing room attendant and tore down the Welsh flag hanging from the home-team balcony. The unsavoury incident did have some positive spin-offs as it helped to consolidate support for the club from the true enthusiasts, who had admired the play of the Gloucestershire team, and the Welsh county also received many sympathetic messages from supporters who had been embarrassed by this tiny group of drunken louts.

A few weeks after their dramatic exit from the competition, Glamorgan played a remarkable Championship game at Colwyn Bay against Nottinghamshire. Having opted to bat first, the visitors slumped to 9-6 in the first 10 overs, with Steve Watkin taking 5 wickets without conceding a run in 21 balls. They subsequently recovered thanks to a belligerent 78 by Alex Wharf, whose brave counter-attack so impressed Matthew Maynard that at the end of the season, Wharf was offered a contract by Glamorgan when he was released by the Trent Bridge club.

After eventually dismissing the Nottinghamshire batsmen for 228, Steve James put their bowlers to the sword, scoring a superb 259*, which at the time was the highest post-war score by a Glamorgan batsman. It was also his fifth century in successive games against Nottinghamshire, and his fourth double hundred for Glamorgan, equalling the club record set by Javed Miandad.

James shared partnerships of 216 for the second wicket with Jacques Kallis, followed by 281 for the third wicket with Mike Powell. When Powell was dismissed for 164 with the score on 503-3, the Nottinghamshire bowlers did not get any respite as Matthew Maynard trotted down the steps of the Rhos-on-Sea pavilion, and then played a little

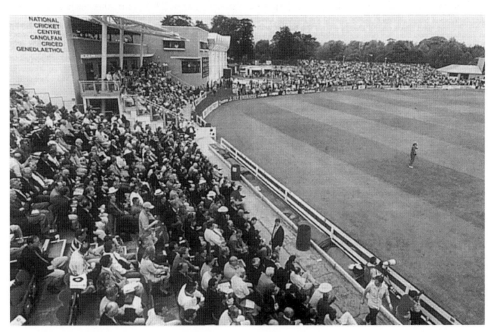

A capacity crowd for the World Cup match at Cardiff in 1999.

Jacques Kallis.

Jeff Hammond.

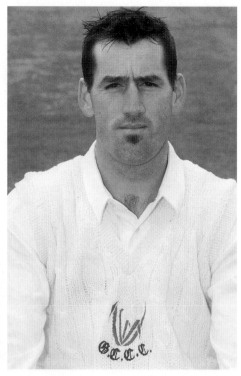

Matthew Elliott.

cameo of an innings, smashing 81 off just 59 balls, to take Glamorgan past 600 for the first time in their history. Maynard eventually declared the innings on 648-4 before Robert Croft took 5-60 to give Glamorgan an innings victory that lifted them off the bottom of the county table.

Steve James was the only Glamorgan batsman to score 1,000 runs in the Championship as 1999 proved to be another summer of unfulfilled promise. Early season progress was also thwarted by injuries, especially captain Matthew Maynard who missed seven weeks after breaking a finger in a fielding practice at the close of play after the first day of the first home Championship match, and then when Maynard was sidelined, vice-captain Steve James sustained a broken thumb. Robert Croft was another key player to be absent as he was on World Cup duty until England departed from the competition at the end of May.

Another person to get an England call-up was Duncan Fletcher. No sooner than returning from his sojourn in 1998 for the first year of his new three-year agreement, the inspirational Glamorgan coach was being linked with the vacant England post. He was eventually approached and appointed from 1 October, with Glamorgan agreeing to release him from his contract with the club. It was typical of the man that he remained loyal to Glamorgan and saw out his summer with the club.

In September Glamorgan announced that Hansie Cronje, the South African captain, had agreed to a two-year appointment as the County's coach. He seemed eager to escape from the politically charged atmosphere in the Cape, and verbally accepted the post, but he subsequently had a change of heart after discussions with the South African cricket authorities who believed that joining the Welsh county would affect his commitments with the national side. Former Australian captain Greg Chappell was the next man to be tipped for the job, but at the end of the day it was Jeff Hammond, another former Australian Test cricketer, who was appointed as Glamorgan's first-team coach for 2000 and 2001. Hammond came with a good track record of success in Australian domestic

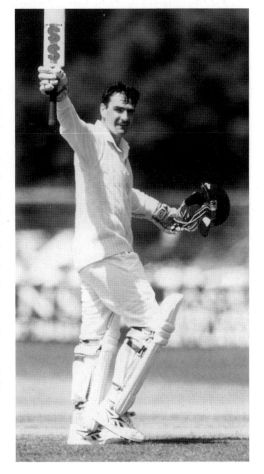

Steve James acknowledging applause after another 100 for Glamorgan.

cricket, having taken South Australia to the final of the Sheffield Shield in 1995 before winning it in 1996.

Another Australian joined the staff for 2000 following the signing of Matthew Elliott, the talented left-handed opener as the County's overseas player and Steve James' opening partner. It was hoped that his acquisition would help to fill the void at the top of the order left by Hugh Morris' retirement at the end of 1997, and it was not long before observers of Glamorgan cricket were pointing out that the last time Steve James had opened on a regular basis with an experienced left-hander, Glamorgan had lifted the Championship and reached the semi-final stages of the NatWest Trophy.

Elliott was also very upbeat about joining Glamorgan, 'My aim is simple – to help Glamorgan win promotion from Division Two of the Championship and to have a run in the one-day tournaments. I was dropped by Australia for the Fourth Test against West Indies last year and did not make it for the recent series against India. I now just want to prove a success for the County – or should that be country, as it is Wales!'

Hopes were therefore high for 2000, and they proved to be well founded as Glamorgan played in a one-day final at Lord's for the first time since 1977, and finally laid to rest the semi-final gremlins that had previously affected them and had seen the NatWest tie with Gloucestershire end so disappointingly.

Matthew Maynard.

11

Lord's at Last

October and November 1999 saw Cardiff and the Welsh Rugby Union play host to the Rugby World Cup. The final was staged at the impressive Millennium Stadium, and after some negotiations, Sophia Gardens was used as an area for a huge tented village where the competition's sponsors could entertain their guests. As Len Smith, Glamorgan's groundsman, and his team started work preparing wickets for the forthcoming season, they found that the huge marquee had caused the grass to wither and despite precautions having been taken, it looked as if lasting damage had been caused to the Sophia Gardens pitch.

As the Glamorgan players and new coach Jeff Hammond gathered at Cardiff for their pre-season training, it looked as if the club had been dealt another hammer blow, even before the first ball had been bowled. But thanks to the hard work of the ground staff, the damage was repaired, new grass was sown and the wickets were ready by the time Maynard and his team began their season in the resurrected zonal rounds of the Benson & Hedges Cup.

They began with a rain-affected contest against Gloucestershire, and despite being shortened to 25 overs, this game set the pattern and established the tactics upon which Glamorgan reached Lord's for the first time since 1977. After Gloucestershire had been restricted to 148-6, Robert Croft and Matthew Elliott launched the Welsh reply with a brisk opening partnership of 59, as Croft proved his worth as a pinch-hitter, exploiting the fact that fielding restrictions were in operation for the first 15 overs. His elevation meant that Steve James dropped into the middle order, and after his success as an opener, a few people wondered whether this would work. But the Gloucestershire match saw James come in at number 6, and he finished as the side's top scorer as Glamorgan won by three wickets with two balls in hand – a victory that proved the mantra of Duncan Fletcher that 'one-day matches are not won by the team that hits the most boundaries, but by the team that accumulates the most singles and twos.'

The following day Glamorgan were defeated on a slow, green wicket at Worcester, before a mix of April showers and heavier pulses of rain caused the abandonment of the zonal games against Somerset and Warwickshire. But every cloud has a silver lining, as the interference of weather meant that Glamorgan could still qualify for the quarter-final stage if they defeated Northamptonshire and improved their net run-rate.

The game saw a fine all-round display from Maynard's team, with Mike Powell adding 74 for the third wicket with the captain, before Dale and James gave the innings a vital late impetus with a stand of 73 in just ten overs to take Glamorgan to 238-8. However, it looked for a while early on as if this might not be enough as Matthew Hayden started to tuck into the Welsh bowling, sweeping Robert Croft for one mighty six high over

The Glamorgan squad of 2000, from left to right, back row: Alun Evans, Wayne Law, Alex Wharf, Simon Jones, David Harrison, Andrew Davies, Mark Wallace. Middle row: Adrian Shaw, Keith Newell, Owen Parkin, Mike Powell, Dean Cosker, Byron Denning (First XI scorer). Front row: Matthew Elliott, Steve Watkin, Steve James, Matthew Maynard, Robert Croft, Adrian Dale, Darren Thomas.

deep square-leg. But he attempted one lusty blow too many as Croft gained his revenge, bowling the Australian with one of his 24-yard specialities that the wily spinner had added to his game.

RDBC – *After playing for England, many people said that I needed more variation, and that's what I did over the winter months. You can either wallow in self-pity or look at yourself in the mirror and think about what you can do to address that. I did that with my batting a few years ago, and over the winter I did the same with my bowling, learning how to mix it up and not let the batsmen settle.*

I had noticed that Hayden was starting to look to hit a boundary off the first couple of balls of each over, and then milk the bowling for the rest of the over. He had already smashed me for one six, so at the start of the next over, I thought I would try something different. I was pleased that it came off as Hayden was, I felt, the man who could have won that game for Northants.

The plucky off-spinner held his nerve as other Northants batsmen tried to up the tempo, and Croft was a worthy Man of the Match as Glamorgan won by 39 runs. An added bonus was that their victory took Glamorgan to the top of their group, and they secured a home quarter-final tie with Hampshire. Much was made in the media in the days leading up to the match at Cardiff about the damage caused by the rugby marquee, so after winning the toss, visiting captain Robin Smith seemed to be wary of batting first on the surface, and asked Glamorgan to bat first, hoping that his bowlers could exploit the overcast conditions and any gremlins in the wicket. His decision seemed to be vindicated as Peter Hartley and Dimitri Mascarenhas reduced Glamorgan to 31-3, but Adrian Dale and Keith Newell then applied themselves carefully to share a partnership of 99 to take Glamorgan to 182-6.

MPM – I felt that this was a more than useful score on a wicket which was never easy to bat on. Steve Watkin and Owen Parkin both bowled a superb spell with the new ball and gave the Hampshire batsmen little width. They eventually perished trying to force the pace rather than working the ball around as Adrian and Keith had done.

Parkin finished with figures of 8-4-16-3, whilst Watkin had the remarkable analysis of 7-5-3-2 as Hampshire subsided to 15-5, before Adrian Dale came on to pick up two wickets as Glamorgan won by the comprehensive margin of 113 runs. As the crowd gathered under the pavilion balcony at Sophia Gardens, the victorious Glamorgan team gathered in their dressing room and gave a loud rendition of their new team song.

OTP – This was something that Matthew Elliott had introduced into our dressing room. Having a song that you sing after victory is something of a club ritual in Australia. Each side has their own, and they take immense pleasure in singing it, especially as the opposition are normally in the next room, separated only by a thin wall! As we sat

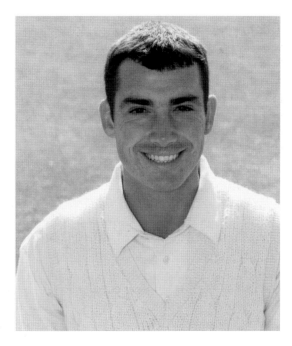

Keith Newell.

A delighted Owen Parkin – a successful bowler and the author of the lyrics in the team song.

around early in the season watching the rain fall, Matthew Elliott came up with the idea that we should have one, so I, having made up a few quirky songs about players in the past, was asked to come up with the words, as soon as possible i.e. overnight! I had a quick bath and soon came up with these lyrics – the tune is like the verses of 'Glory, Glory, Man. United', which the football supporters sing at Old Trafford:

> *Over the Severn and down to the Taff,*
> *Like lambs to the slaughter, they take on the Daff.*
> *Now do they know how hard the Welsh we fight,*
> *As they trudge back to England beaten out of sight!*
>
> *We are Glamorgan, dragons you and me,*
> *Together we stand as the pride of Cymru,*
> *We play to conquer, we play to thrill,*
> *We play for the glory of the mighty Daffodil.*

The team's reward was their first semi-final in the competition for 12 years, and a home tie with Surrey. With ten international cricketers in their ranks, the visitors were the firm favourites before the start of the match, but Glamorgan turned the tables on their illustrious opponents with another confident all-round display, and a memorable display of batting from Matthew Maynard. Persistent rain in the build-up to the game and on the Saturday morning meant that play was delayed until 4 p.m., and then in the 24.1 overs that were possible, Glamorgan, having won the toss, lost Croft and Elliott early, before Powell and Maynard steadied the ship to take the side to 99-2 when play was called off for the day.

MJP – *I was really nervous before batting in the Surrey match and when I got out there I just tried to concentrate on every ball, and pick up a few singles here and there. But when you've got Matt, who is one of the best players in the country, at the other end that helps to take the pressure off. All I had to do was play around him whilst he was hitting fours and sixes.*

I love batting with Matt – he's always very calm and full of good advice. Our styles also compliment each other – I'm very much a front foot player, whilst Matt's so good

A watchful Matthew Maynard.

Above left: Alex Wharf.
Above right: Matthew Maynard – the Man of the Match in the 2000 final.

off the back foot. It means that bowlers never really get a chance to settle into a steady length when we're batting together.

The wicket against Surrey was a low and skiddy one, and not really suited to the bowling of Tudor or Bicknell, so when Maynard and Powell resumed their partnership the following morning, Maynard showing great responsibility with a chanceless century, adding 133 in 27 overs with his partner, before falling for 109 from 115 balls.

After Matthew's dismissal, a little bit of panic set in and Glamorgan lost their last six wickets for 25 runs. With Surrey's impressive line-up, it seemed as if the hard work of Powell and Maynard might have all been in vain, but Owen Parkin made two early breakthroughs dismissing Ali Brown and Alex Tudor. Mark Butcher and Alec Stewart then restored Surrey's fortunes before Butcher fell to a superb stumping by Adrian Shaw off Croft's clever spin-bowling – a feat that the Glamorgan wicketkeeper was to repeat a few days later in Glamorgan's tourist match against the West Indians when Shaw stumped the illustrious Brian Lara.

Alex Wharf then bowled perhaps the most decisive spell of the contest, ripping the heart out of Surrey's middle order by dismissing both the Hollioake brothers and Graham Thorpe.

AGW – *It was great to be part of the success – good to be selected and good to do well. There was never a chance that Surrey could have pulled it back. They were too far behind and we were on so much of a high and playing well as a unit. It was also good to play in front of so many people who are willing you to do well.*

After another interruption for rain, Martin Bicknell, Jason Ratcliffe and Alex Stewart attempted a late rally, but Parkin still had three overs up his sleeve and he came back to finish things off. When Steve James held onto a lob from Bicknell, Glamorgan had won by 32 runs under the Duckworth-Lewis method, and their victory was accompanied by scenes of sheer euphoria as the players gathered on the balcony of the Cardiff pavilion, whilst below their ecstatic supporters celebrated as if the Cup had actually been lifted rather than Glamorgan having at long last reached a final at Lord's.

OTP – *It was an emotional roller coaster. I broke through twice in two balls early on, including Ali Brown that was most pleasing. At one stage, I had bowled 5 overs for 14 runs – but my final figures were 8.4 overs for 64 runs, so 22 balls yielded 50 runs! I knew the Surrey batsmen were going to slog me because they needed 12 an over and it was just a case of keeping the ball full. I was waiting for them to miss-hit, but I have to say a few of the balls went straight back over my head for six. On days like that it's a case of just trying to keep going and keeping your discipline – even though you know you might end up being hit back over your head. It was immense relief that greeted me when 'Jamer' held onto Alec Stewart at mid-wicket and then the jubilation*

The Glamorgan players leave the field after beating Surrey at Cardiff.

'We've done it' – the Glamorgan team celebrate reaching the Benson & Hedges final in 2000.

followed. All the boys were jumping for joy in the changing room but I was sat quietly, a light shade of green. I guess I knew how close we and in fact I had got to going down in history books for the wrong reasons!

SLW – When Surrey were seven wickets down, a few of the senior players said 'We've been here before and we're not going to let it slip again.' When Alec Stewart started firing boundaries, my mind did race back to Hove in 1993. We knew though that we just had to stay composed and not crack. Fortunately, Parky came through and got a couple of wickets at the end. We've been close in the past, but the main difference in 2000 was that we were so much more relaxed about things – before there had been a huge build-up with meetings about the side we were playing. Then when we went out there we were too anxious. This time, we concentrated on what we did best and stuck to a well-organised game-plan.

RDBC – One of the things I'll always remember from that game happened before the start, when we were all lined up to have our photographs taken for the match programme in case we got through to the final. As I was standing there, one of the Surrey boys walked past and said 'Hey, you don't need those. You're not going to get to the final.' He might have said it with his tongue in his cheek, but even so, it was really great to prove him wrong and get to the final at Lord's.

For the next few weeks, cricket enthusiasts and sports fans all over South Wales started to make their arrangements for 12 June, and the media spotlight was placed on Matthew Maynard and his team.

The team enjoy a raucous rendition of their new team song, written by Owen Parkin (front left).

MJP – *It was quite a strange feeling in the days leading up to the match when complete strangers came up to wish us good luck. The day before the match we had a different pattern to normal by travelling by coach up to London, then when we got to Lord's we had the home dressing room, where few of us had ever been before.*

12 June 2000 was 'Daffodil Day' as over 15,000 Welsh supporters descended from far and wide to make Lord's seem more like Cardiff Arms Park for a rugby international. All were hopeful that this would be the day when Matthew Maynard would take a piece of silverware back to Wales, from the very heart of English cricket. It seemed as if the script was going according to plan as Maynard won the toss and thousands of patriotic Welsh voices roared in approval as Matt Elliott and Robert Croft walked out to start the Glamorgan innings.

RDBC – *I'd never heard anything quite like it on any cricket field I have played on. It was a wonderful feeling and as I took strike the hairs were standing up on the back of my neck.*

But within the space of a few overs, both openers were back in the pavilion, the Glamorgan captain found himself at the crease in a major game with Mike Powell, and the pair repeated their Herculean efforts in the semi-final by adding 137 in 31 overs.

MJP – *I had never seen so many at a cricket match before, and it was amazing to walk out to bat with so many people cheering you. Matt's knock was awesome – he kept chipping good balls from Snape and the others through mid-wicket for one's and two's, and then when the bad ball came along, he smashed it for four. As Matt reached fifty, a huge roar went up. It was so loud I had goosebumps all over. Then people*

The Lord's scoreboard early on in the partnership between Maynard and Powell.

starting singing 'Bread of Heaven' and other rugby songs, and I went down the wicket to Matt and said 'Can you hear that – isn't it brilliant.'

MPM – Mike was quite tense at first and Mike Smith sensed his anxiety by calling for a short-leg. Gradually he relaxed and started letting the ball come on to his bat. The runs started to come and we pushed Gloucestershire onto the defensive. I had started very quietly, content to push the singles, before finding my stride. The crowd was unlike anything I had ever experienced – when I reached my half-century our supporters started singing 'Hymns and Arias' and I had to compose myself for a couple of deliveries, overcome by emotion. Afterwards many of the Benson & Hedges reps said that there had been many better games of cricket in the final, but that there had never been an atmosphere quite like that one.

Maynard was not content with a cameo half-century, and he continued with his master-class in the art of disciplined batting, and was well on course towards a treasured century when Powell was caught and bowled by Jeremy Snape with the score on 161-2. There were still plenty of overs in hand for the other Glamorgan batsmen to give Maynard further support, but nobody was able to hang around as Maynard reached his coveted century – it was the first time any batsman had scored a century in both the semi-final and final of a domestic one-day competition.

Despite Matthew's sterling efforts, Glamorgan's innings fell away, as Harvey returned to strangle the lower order, and Maynard was run out in the final over after a direct hit by Kim Barnett. As the Glamorgan walked off there was a standing ovation, and hand-shakes from all of the Gloucestershire fielders.

RDBC – *Matthew's knock was a truly great one – especially under the pressure of playing in a final and in front of such a huge crowd. The effort and commitment that the whole Glamorgan team showed was fantastic. Instead of lying down we fought all the way. I always thought that if we got somewhere in the region of 225 to 240 we would compete, but unfortunately we didn't quite pull it off.*

Even Glamorgan's most fervent supporters knew in their heart of hearts that their side had finished twenty or thirty runs short of a decent score, so fingers were crossed that the Glamorgan bowlers, who had done so much to get the side to Lord's, would come up trumps again. Unfortunately, Tim Hancock and the vastly experienced Kim Barnett feasted on the Glamorgan attack, and when Robert Croft was introduced in the 14th over, Gloucestershire already had 72 runs on the board.

MPM – *I still felt 225 was a reasonable target and that we had a good chance of defending it. But we had to excel in the bowling department, and it just was not their day. We had developed an excellent one-day formula, and Steve Watkin and Owen Parkin had got us to the final with their performances against Hampshire and Surrey. For once, they could not do the trick for us. I am not sure if it was nerves. Steve had looked forward to the moment of walking out on the Lord's field for a number of years and I think he was feeling the moment when he dropped his first delivery short.*

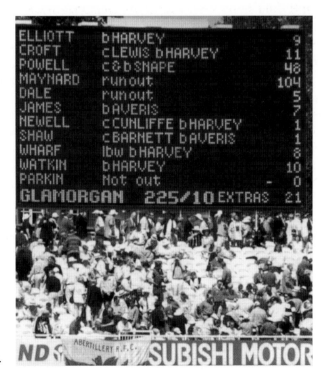

The end of the innings.

Left: Matthew Maynard celebrates at Lord's after reaching 100.
Right: Robert Croft.

SLW – *I had an off day in those opening ten overs. Lord's can be a funny place to bowl, especially with its slope, and perhaps the mistake I made was not pushing harder to play there the previous week when we were at Lord's for a Sunday match, and to have built up some rhythm and get used to the ground.*

OTP – *The final at Lords was a fantastic experience and although we were never really in the game, I shall always look back with delight. They had targeted the first ten overs of their innings as a time to get after us and it really did come off. I have watched that opening spell numerous times now on video and I still do not feel that I bowled particularly badly – it just seemed to go their way!*

Gloucestershire's scoring rate steadily dropped, and in trying to force the pace, Barnett played on to Croft. Steve Watkin returned to take the wicket of Rob Cunliffe, and when Owen Parkin pulled off a spectacular catch off his own bowling, Gloucestershire had slipped to 131-3 after 30 overs. But any thoughts of a Welsh victory were finally extinguished by a brisk partnership of 95 in 17 overs by Matt Windows and captain Mark Alleyne.

ADS – *As Gloucestershire got closer and closer to their target, I kept thinking I'll probably never get another chance to play in a final at Lord's, so I said to Mark*

Alleyne, 'Booboo, can I have one of these stumps at the end?' He asked me which one I wanted. I said middle stump, so a few minutes later, when the winning runs were struck, Alleyne grabbed the leg and off stump out of the ground and said to me, 'There you are Shawsy, the middle one is all yours. It's now one of my proudest possessions.

Gloucestershire's victory by seven wickets, achieved with nineteen balls in hand, was their third successive victory in a one-day final. However, it was Maynard who was the unanimous choice as Man of the Match after his vintage display of cultured stroke play.

Opposite: Owen Parkin and the Glamorgan team celebrate a wicket.

Matthew Elliott batting for Glamorgan.

MPM – *I found it hard to smile when I was given the award because what I had really wanted to be presented with was the Benson & Hedges Cup. Perhaps when I have retired I will be able to look back on the award more fondly, but I would far rather have scored a duck and been on the winning side. Cricket is a team game. It is made up of individuals and it relies on individual performances, but at the end of the day, it is about how the team does, not you.*

The game was won and lost in twenty overs – the last ten in our innings when we lost eight wickets and the first ten in theirs when they hit a number of boundaries. It was very disappointing, but the experience of playing in a one-day final is something that every player wants to repeat. We sat in the dressing room for what seemed like hours after the presentation ceremony. That hollow feeling that defeat brings takes more than a few drinks afterwards to fill. We had been beaten by the better team on the day, but that did not make the pain any less acute, especially our feelings for our magnificent supporters – they had transformed St John's Wood into Little Wales for the weekend.

It wasn't long though, before Glamorgan had got the winning habit back as July saw Maynard's team record a sequence of four successive Championship victories – it was the first time since 1968 that they had won four games in a row. The sequence began at Swansea with Glamorgan, languishing at the bottom of the Division Two, without a win to their name, taking on Worcestershire, who were at the top of the table. The Welsh county turned the form book on its head, as Darren Thomas claimed eight wickets and Dean Cosker five as Worcestershire failed by 82 runs to chase a target of 334 on the final day.

It only looked like a temporary upswing in the County's fortunes as they travelled to Northampton for the next game without either Maynard and Croft, who were both on one-day duty with England. These worst fears seemed confirmed as Glamorgan slumped to 77 for 6 at lunch on the first day, but after the interval Alex Wharf completely changed the complexion of the game firstly, with a superb hundred – his first in the Championship – and then the burly all-rounder tore in with the new ball and took three wickets as Northants slumped to 85-7. After some brief tail-end resistance, Elliott and acting captain James extended the lead and Northants were left needing 323 to win. But they were never in the hunt against another display of spirited Welsh bowling, with Watkin and Thomas each claiming three wickets as Glamorgan won by 144 runs.

Steve Watkin.

153

Above: Adrian Shaw.
Opposite page: Matthew Elliott hits a legside four at Cardiff.

The sequence of victories was maintained as Glamorgan made their first visit to Southgate, still without Maynard and Croft, and now without Watkin who was injured prior to the start of the game. The pattern of success was also changed as Glamorgan had to bat last and chase a target of 307 on a pitch that had seen 17 wickets fall on the first day and had resulted in an apparently hasty decision by the ECB pitch inspectors to dock Middlesex eight points. But this was all history as far as the Glamorgan batsmen were concerned as they began their run-chase on the third evening, with James and Elliott carefully taking the score to 69 for 0 at the close.

Middlesex had an early success on the final morning as James was dismissed by Phil Tufnell, but Elliott was unperturbed and the Australian reached three figures with a mighty six off the former England spinner. With 76 still required, Elliott was stumped and the loss of further wickets caused nerve ends to jangle. But Shaw and Thomas held their nerve, and took Glamorgan to a deserved two-wicket win – their first on Middlesex soil since 1954.

Maynard, Croft and Watkin were all restored to the Glamorgan side for the next game against Northamptonshire at Cardiff, with Watkin taking his 800th first-class wicket before pulling up with a groin strain after bowling just eight overs. In his absence Darren Thomas rose to the occasion, taking 5-43, but Glamorgan then surrendered the advantage and Northants had an invaluable 31-run lead on a wicket that was expected to help the spinners on the final day. Robert Croft, who had been released early from the England one-day squad, bowled a disciplined spell as the Northants batsmen tried to build a sizeable lead.

David Ripley and Tony Penberthy then shared a stubborn partnership, adding 64 for the seventh wicket, and it looked as if they would take the game out of Glamorgan's reach. But Adrian Dale took a fine tumbling catch to dismiss Ripley, and Croft quickly polished off the tail to leave Glamorgan needing 309. They suffered an early blow when they lost Steve James with just 36 runs on the board, but for the second successive game, Elliott led a spirited run-chase on the final day with the Australian using his tall reach to nullify the spin of Jason Brown and Graeme Swann. By the time he was eventually out for 117, he had put Glamorgan into a winning position, and despite another mid-innings wobble Keith Newell and Adrian Shaw saw Glamorgan home with five wickets in hand.

The winning sequence had seen Glamorgan rise from the bottom of Division Two to the top of the table, and all with a game in hand over their nearest rivals. But any thoughts of extending the lead were quickly dispelled as the winning run ended in the

Steve James and Matthew Elliott in front of the Colwyn Bay scoreboard after their record-breaking stand against Sussex in 2000.

next game on an indifferent wicket at Bristol as Gloucestershire beat the Welsh side for the first time since 1989.

But Glamorgan got back into winning habits at the end of August as for the second successive year they travelled to North Wales to play Sussex in what turned out to be a quite remarkable record-breaking game. Visiting captain Chris Adams was aware of how capricious the Rhos wicket had been on the opening day the previous summer, and with the wicket looking quite green again, he invited Glamorgan to bat after winning the toss. It was not long before he must have been regretting his decision, as the home side reached 457-1 by the close of play, with Steve James and Matt Elliott adding a record 374 for the first wicket.

Once again Steve James found Colwyn Bay to be a happy hunting ground as he continued his productive sequence on the Rhos wicket, and inflicted further punishment on the weary Sussex bowlers, as he went on to score 309* and record the first-ever triple hundred in Glamorgan's history, after over nine hours at the crease to break Emrys Davies' previous best of 287* made back in 1939.

SPJ – *The wicket is always a decent one up at Colwyn Bay, and it's probably good for me that the square boundaries are quite short! That particular year, I was in a bit of a bad run before going up north and after being out for a duck in the previous one-day game, I had spent the day before the Sussex match all on my own fretting about how to bat the next day.*

However, I immediately felt in good nick, and reached 193* by the end of the first day. I was physically tired, but there were lots of things running through my mind. I had got 259 the previous year, and had my eye on 300. I got various messages as well on my mobile wishing me luck, including one from Alan Jones saying 'Well played and go on and get 300.'

Things continued to go my way the next morning, and by the afternoon I was closing in on the record. As I moved into the 290s, the pressure started to build up and the runs also dried up. Then when I was on 296, I saw the scoreboard operator put a ladder up, ready to climb up and take down the '2' and replace it with a '3'. I thought if that isn't tempting fate I don't know what is! Soon afterwards, I smashed one thinking I had done it, but then one of the Sussex boys made a fine stop in the covers, and I thought crickey, I'm not going to do it. But eventually I managed to nudge a couple around and then nurdle one from Umer Rashid to get past 300.

Lots of very nice things were said afterwards and the next morning I was really touched to get a letter from Peter Davies, Emrys' son, congratulating me on reaching the milestone. Emrys, like Alan Jones, was a very fine player and they both played their cricket when games were over three days, and on uncovered wickets. Nowadays, the four-day matches are on flatter wickets, and I'm very lucky to get the opportunities to play long innings when others before me did not.

James' steadfast innings also saw the Glamorgan reach a total of 718-3 – the highest in the club's history. The visitors were naturally quite weary after a day and a half of leather chasing, and they did quite well to amass 342, with both Adams and Rashid recording hundreds. In a normal game this might have been sufficient to avoid the follow-on, but this was not the case in this game, and they went in again still 376 runs behind. Within eight

Emrys Davies.

overs, both of their openers were back in the pavilion, and although Adams and Robin Martin-Jenkins both offered valiant resistance, it was really only a matter of time before Glamorgan were able to celebrate victory. In the end, it was Adrian Dale who hastened Sussex's demise, with a return of 5-46. As the Sussex players headed home, they must have wondered how many other teams had scored over 300 in each innings, yet still lost by an innings.

This proved to be Glamorgan's final Championship success of the summer, but it was sufficient to see the County win promotion into Division One. It was a worthy reward after the disappointments of Lord's and the celebrations on the Sophia Gardens balcony after securing ten points in the final game against Middlesex also marked the end of Matthew Maynard's term as the club captain. Right from the onset of the summer, he had said that this would be his final year in charge of the team.

The final Championship match of the summer epitomised Maynard's approach to captaincy as his bowlers strived for the bonus points that would secure promotion. His approach to leadership, just like his batting, had always been to trust his instincts and as Glamorgan's progress was being thwarted by a stubborn partnership, he decided to bring on the occasional seam bowling of Keith Newell. It did the trick as Newell took a wicket in his first over, and the Middlesex resistance soon ended, allowing Glamorgan to celebrate promotion to Division One of the County Championship.

Glamorgan in the Benson & Hedges Cup – 2000

ZONAL ROUNDS

15 April at Sophia Gardens, Cardiff
Gloucestershire 148-6 in 25 overs (M.W. Alleyne 50, S.L. Watkin 3-7)
Glamorgan 150-7 in 24.4 overs (S.P .James 34, M.W. Alleyne 2-28, K.J. Barnett 2-28)
Glamorgan won by 3 wickets

16 April at Worcester
Glamorgan 147 in 46.4 overs (A. Dale 49*, Kabir Ali 4-29, S.R. Lampitt 2-16,
   D.A. Leatherdale 2-23)
Worcestershire 148-1 in 29.4 overs (P.R. Pollard 54*, G.A. Hick 55*)
Worcestershire won by 9 wickets

19 April at Taunton
Somerset v. Glamorgan
Match Abandoned

22 April at Sophia Gardens, Cardiff
Glamorgan v. Warwickshire
Match Abandoned

24 April at Northampton
Glamorgan 238-8 in 50 overs (M.P. Maynard 48, D.M. Cousins 3-36)
Northamptonshire 199 in 46 overs (M.L. Hayden 67, S.D. Thomas 3-49, A. Dale 2-37)
Glamorgan won by 39 runs

QUARTER-FINAL

9 May at Sophia Gardens, Cardiff
Glamorgan 182-6 in 50 overs (A. Dale 63, K. Newell 49, P.J. Hartley 2-22)
Hampshire 69 in 34.2 overs (O.T. Parkin 3-18, S.L. Watkin 2-3, A. Dale 2-11,
   K. Newell 2-6)
Glamorgan won by 113 runs

SEMI-FINAL

27-28 May at Sophia Gardens, Cardiff
Glamorgan 251 in 49.1 overs (M.P. Maynard 109, M.J. Powell 67, A.J. Hollioake 3-36)
Surrey 212 in 43 overs (A.J. Stewart 85, O.T. Parkin 4-60, A.G. Wharf 3-37,
   R.D.B. Croft 3-42)
Glamorgan won by 32 runs (D/L Method)

FINAL

10 June at Lord's
Glamorgan 225 in 49.3 overs (M.P. Maynard 104, M.J. Powell 48, I.J. Harvey 5-34)
Gloucestershire 226-3 in 46.5 overs (T.H.C. Hancock 60, M.G.N. Windows 53*)
Gloucestershire won by 7 wickets

12

2001 – An Up and Down Sort of Year

Steve James was the man chosen to step into Matthew Maynard's shoes as the County's new leader. He inherited from Matthew Maynard a talented squad that had made considerable progress after the lows of the mid-1990s, with the Championship success in 1997 and the run in the Benson & Hedges competition in 2000 both giving the players the sweet taste of success, and creating an air of expectation within the club's corridors of power. Previous changes of captaincy had been during a trough of despair or in the midst of a poor run of form. This was not the case for James as he began pre-season training with the rest of the squad, and the fact that he went on to guide the club to further success in League cricket in both 2001 and 2002 speaks volumes for the abilities of the Lydney-born opener.

The immediate targets for James' team at the start of the 2001 season were to aim for a top three spot in Division One of the Championship and to press for further success in the one-day competitions. Despite their appearance at Lord's, the Glamorgan Dragons had enjoyed rather indifferent form in the National League of 2000, and they had failed to match promotion in the Championship with a move into Division One of the National League. There was a feeling though that Glamorgan were basically a good one-day side, and with Matthew Elliott unable to return for 2001, the club replaced him with another Australian – Jimmy Maher, the twenty-seven-year-old opener from Queensland who was regarded as the best one-day cricketer in Australia.

Maher quickly adjusted to the demands of English wickets, and in early May the Queenslander struck a fine 142* against Gloucestershire in the zonal rounds of the Benson & Hedges competition. But just as they had relied on an individual performance at Lord's the year before, no other Glamorgan batsman went past 30, and on the easy-paced wicket, Gloucestershire's batsmen reached their target of 237 with nine balls to spare.

To make matters worse, Stephen James suffered a knee injury during the game at Bristol, and the Glamorgan captain was on the sidelines as his team went on to lose all of their games in the 50-overs competition, and swiftly exited from the competition. There was little joy in the NatWest Trophy either, where after beating Derbyshire at Cardiff, Glamorgan went down to a seven-wicket defeat in the fourth round at Taunton, as Somerset's Marcus Trescothick tore the Glamorgan attack apart, scoring a scintillating 121 off 83 balls, including 20 fours.

The Norwich Union game at Old Trafford on 20 May saw Glamorgan open their one-day account for the season, and almost by accident, they discovered a winning formula that was to stand them in great stead for the rest of the season, and beyond.

Jimmy Maher on the balcony at Cardiff after Glamorgan had won Division Two of the National League, with Darren Thomas (left) and Steve James (right).

SPJ – *It was not the greatest of wickets and with Murali in the Lancashire team, we felt that our best chance of winning was to whack as many as possible in the first 15 overs when the fielding restrictions were operating. Keith Newell went in first with Jimmy Maher, and Crofty came in at number 3. It can be a high-risk strategy if the ball is moving around, but this time it worked a treat, so we decided to stick with it for the next few games – after more success, it turned out to be our game plan for the rest of the season.*

At the end of May, Glamorgan had also suffered a heavy defeat in the Championship encounter with Yorkshire at Swansea, where the Tykes won by 328 runs, and with Glamorgan at the bottom of the Division One table in the Championship, it seemed as if from a playing point of view 2001 was going to be a season of despair for James and his team. Team morale though was still high, despite the lack of Championship success, and after scoring his maiden Championship century in the away match against Kent, Jimmy Maher brought his own touch of Australian humour to proceedings.

MPM – *Jimmy had been in high spirits all week, especially after Australia had bowled England out for 86 at Old Trafford. Jimmy had been travelling with me, but after we arrived at our hotel, Jimmy disappeared. The lads told me that he had popped down to the ground apparently to work on his batting with Jeff Hammond, but when we got there the next morning, we found that Jimmy had been decorating the dressing room green and gold. Not only this, he had got every press cutting from every paper that*

*mentioned the Australians' victory and stuck them up in our dressing room as well.
It brought a huge smile to the boy's faces when we saw what Jimmy had done!*

In early June, the Glamorgan team got back into winning ways with two astonishing back-to-back wins against Essex at Chelmsford. In the Championship encounter, they recovered from a sticky start on the first day, thanks to a seventh wicket stand of 163 by Adrian Dale and Darren Thomas. Both batsmen scored hundreds, and in the case of Thomas' career-best 138 it was also his maiden first-class hundred, and the highest individual score by a Glamorgan number 8, eclipsing Malcolm Nash's 130 against Surrey in 1976.

Thomas then took four wickets as the Glamorgan attack forced Essex to follow-on for the fourth match in succession. But their batsmen showed greater resilience batting for a second time and with Paul Grayson making a watchful 189, Essex had reached 540-7 when Ronnie Irani declared, setting Glamorgan a seemingly improbable 364 to win from 84 overs.

In their entire history, Glamorgan had only once before reached such a mammoth target batting second in a Championship game, but this was not in the minds of Steve James and Matthew Maynard as they launched an astonishing run-chase on the final afternoon. The two captains, past and present, shared a rollicking partnership of 194 in just 38 overs as every Essex bowler was put to the sword. James eventually fell after a magnificent 156 and whilst Maynard blasted 90 from 115 balls before holing out off Grayson's spin bowling. But any thoughts Essex may have had of snatching a remarkable victory were dispelled as a quickfire 43 from Adrian Dale saw Glamorgan to their first Championship win of the season with 25 balls to spare.

But if this was an audacious display of batting, then the run-chase the following day in the Norwich Union contest against the same opponents simply defied belief, and proved that James' ambitions for the season were not misplaced. But a Glamorgan victory did not look on the cards as Ronnie Irani blasted a

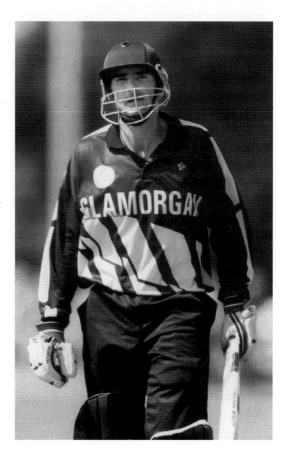

Steve James.

Darren Thomas.

61-ball century after rain had delayed the start. Further interruptions to the weather meant that Glamorgan ended up with a target of 254 in just 34 overs at an asking rate of 7.5 an over.

Keith Newell and Matthew Maynard then responded with another withering assault on the Essex bowlers. Despite the early loss of Jimmy Maher, Glamorgan reached a hundred in just ten overs as Newell galloped to a blistering 97 from just 53 deliveries before being caught by Mark Illot off Justin Bishop's bowling. It was a small crumb of comfort for Illot who earlier in the innings had been smashed for 27 in just one over. But Newell's departure only brought an equally aggressive Mike Powell to the wicket and together with Matthew Maynard they saw Glamorgan home with thirteen balls to spare.

KN – *It was one of those days when it all clicked. I'd started opening the batting in league games on a regular basis the previous year, and had done it before when I was with Sussex. You have to be clued up over your shot selection, especially if you are going to hit over the top. You are bound to get out cheaply now and again. But on that particular day at Chelmsford, everything was in the right slot and everything I tried came off.*

The following weekend at Cardiff, it was the Worcestershire bowlers who were slain by the Dragons batsmen, as Jimmy Maher picked up where his team-mates had left off at Chelmsford, with Maher smashing a superb 94 from 76 balls; together with forceful half-centuries from Robert Croft, who was now batting at number 3 in the order, and Adrian Dale, Glamorgan finished on 305-6, their highest-ever score in League cricket. With Croft in canny mode with the ball, the visiting batsmen were never in the hunt, and Glamorgan recorded another morale-boosting win by 111 runs.

But James' side could not translate their one-day form into the longer form of the game, and whilst they maintained their quest for the Division Two title in the Norwich Union League, they languished in the relegation zone of the First Division of the County Championship. Jimmy Maher and Adrian Dale were the only batsmen to show any consistency, with both men passing a thousand and scoring double-hundreds during the summer. They were also thwarted by bad weather, losing in all over a quarter of all playing time in the four-day games. Injuries to various players also did not help matters, with Jimmy Maher fracturing a finger, Alex Wharf being hampered by various shin and ankle problems, and then when Steve James had recovered from his knee operation, he became another casualty when his hand was fractured at Taunton by his old adversary Andy Caddick.

Wicketkeeper Adrian Shaw was also taken ill before the start of the match against Kent in mid-June, and his wicketkeeping understudy Mark Wallace was summoned from a second-team match at Abergavenny to the Championship match at Maidstone. The former England Under-19 wicketkeeper had previously made his County debut at the end of the 1999 season, and in the match against Somerset at Taunton he had, aged 17 years and 287 days, become Glamorgan's youngest-ever wicketkeeper in Championship cricket. Wallace marked his first-team call-up to Maidstone with a gritty 80, as well as 8 catches, to prove his immense potential, and by the end of the 2001 campaign Wallace had secured a regular place behind the stumps in Glamorgan's Championship side as Adrian Shaw was appointed the 2nd XI captain for 2002.

Wallace's outstanding wicketkeeping was one crumb of comfort as Glamorgan continued to be affected by poor weather in their Championship games. After a monumental thunderstorm had washed

Mark Wallace – Glamorgan's youngest-ever wicketkeeper in Championship cricket.

Keith Newell blasts another boundary.

out play on the second day of the match with Surrey, the rains relented at The Oval to allow Wallace to display his promise with the bat. The nineteen year old scored a mature half-century in Glamorgan's first innings, before the Glamorgan bowlers counter-attacked in Surrey's second innings. Simon Jones ripped out Mark Butcher and Mark Ramprakash as Surrey lurched to 7-2, before Steve Watkin and Andrew Davies filleted the middle order, to leave Glamorgan requiring 200 runs to win.

Surrey had not lost at The Oval for nearly three years, and with their talented attack, Glamorgan had a stiff task on their plate. But after the early loss of Jimmy Maher, Mike Powell and Ian Thomas, the twenty-two-year-old left-hander both scored impressive half-centuries. For Thomas, it was another determined innings for the former UWIC student who had joined the County's full-time staff after impressing whilst on a match contract during the 2000 season. On his first-class debut, he hit a composed 82 against Essex at Southend, and during this particular match at The Oval, Thomas showed great character in compiling a fluent fifty to take his side within sight of their target. Martin Bicknell then took four quick wickets in as many overs to leave the game tantalisingly poised, but Mark Wallace and Andrew Davies ensured that all of the hard work had not been wasted, and they steadied the ship to take Glamorgan to their first win at The Oval for sixteen years.

APD – *I was called up to this game while playing at Usk for the Second XI, and my confidence was not at its highest, especially when walking out at The Oval to see them warming up with eleven internationals in their team. But we played out of our skins, and in our second innings, overcame a slight collapse. It was a bit daunting walking down those famous Oval steps on a pair, but I managed to survive with Wally until tea. I remember the reception Martin Bicknell had at teatime from the Surrey supporters. To them it seemed as if the game was over, and to be honest with nearly forty or fifty to get, who could have blamed them. But it wasn't to be the brown hatters' day as Wally played superbly and perfected the drive through the slips off Saqlain!*

MPM – *To say the victory against Surrey was a good one would be something of an understatement. We played some of the best cricket since 1997. Our bowlers were exceptional, and to bowl a near Test team out twice was a magnificent achievement. They applied great pressure to the Surrey batsmen all the way through, but our victory was not as easy as it seemed at one stage. We slipped to 167-7, but this was the cue for another very important innings from Mark Wallace. His 18 not out may not seem a massive score, but in the context of the game it was huge as he joined forces with Andrew Davies to guide us to victory.*

By this time, Glamorgan were still unbeaten at home in the Norwich Union League and the Dragons added the scalps of the Essex Eagles to their tally in mid-August at Cardiff. On a perfect batting wicket, Keith Newell and Robert Croft were both in awesome form with the bat, with both batsmen scoring attractive half-centuries. After a late flurry from Mike Powell, Glamorgan reached 289-6, before Andrew Davies tore into the heart of the Eagles' batting, with the young swing-bowler taking 5-39 to set up a comprehensive victory by 178 runs.

This victory pushed them up into the top three in Division Two behind leaders Durham Dynamos. At the end of the month, the Dragons met the leaders in a vital match at Cardiff, and for the fifth time in the summer, the batsmen took the total over 250, with Jimmy Maher and Matthew Maynard sharing a quick-fire stand of 71 for the fifth wicket. Nicky Peng, the young Durham opener, then took the attack to the Glamorgan bowlers, but there was only support from captain Jon Lewis. Peng was eventually caught by Maher off Cosker for 92 and once Andrew Davies had dismissed both Lewis and Jimmy Daley, Durham's run-chase had been stifled, and Glamorgan had gained a vital win to take them to the top of the Division Two table.

Two days later, Glamorgan guaranteed promotion into Division One of the Norwich Union League after a vintage display of batting from Matthew Maynard in the day-night encounter against the

Keith Newell.

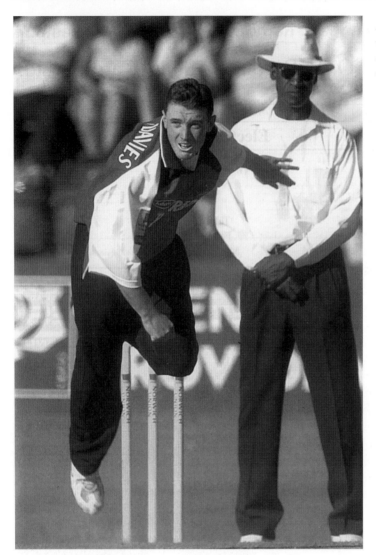

Andrew Davies bowls for Glamorgan, watched by umpire Vanburn Holder.

Hampshire Hawks at Cardiff. Floodlit cricket had been a popular innovation at the Cardiff ground in 2000, with the match against Essex being played in front of a full house at the club's new headquarters. The prospect of seeing the Dragons gain promotion attracted another capacity crowd to Sophia Gardens for the match against the Hawks, and Matthew Maynard responded with an audacious century, reviving memories of his batting at Lord's the previous year.

But at 55-4, it looked as if the Dragons' fine run in League cricket might be coming to an end, but Maynard took the game by the scruff of the neck, to strike an unbeaten 116 – his 14th one-day century for the County and a new Glamorgan record. His 92-run partnership in just 12 overs with Adrian Dale put Glamorgan back into the driving seat, before Robert Croft took 4-33 as the visitors tried to chase the target of 245. Once Croft had dismissed Neil Johnson, the visitors' overseas batsman, the target was out of their reach, and Glamorgan cruised to a 51-run victory that took them four points clear of both Durham and Worcestershire at the top of the table.

After gaining two vital points from the abandoned match at Worcester, the Dragons knew that they would secure the Division Two title if they beat the Sussex Sharks in the next League match in another day-night encounter at Hove. This time, however, they were comprehensively outplayed by the South Coast side, and after the 34-run defeat, Steve James and his men travelled to play a Championship match at Leicester knowing that if Durham beat Worcestershire, Glamorgan would still secure the title. The Championship match ended in another heavy defeat, but Durham came to Glamorgan's aide by defeating Worcestershire, and the Dragons had won Division Two.

Soon afterwards, it was also confirmed that Steve Watkin had been appointed as director of the newly-created Cricket Academy, and the final match of the season against Middlesex at Cardiff was therefore something of a double celebration, as all of the Glamorgan players were eager to mark the day that Steve Watkin brought down the curtain on his distinguished county career, with a performance, as Division Two champions, that they could all take pride in.

As the Glamorgan batsmen went out to bat first, there were plenty of smiles on the faces of the Glamorgan supporters, despite the fact that the results in the day's Championship matches had confirmed Glamorgan's relegation from Division One of the four-day competition. But this was not a day on which to be gloomy, and Robert Croft set the tempo for the subsequent celebrations with his maiden one-day hundred; with Steve James scoring an imperious 93, Middlesex were set a stiff target of 273. They never had a realistic chance after another incisive spell by Andrew Davies and some controlled bowling by Robert Croft and Darren Thomas.

With Glamorgan on the verge of their eighth home win, the game ended in an emotional way as Watkin delivered the final over.

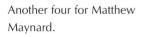

Another four for Matthew Maynard.

Steve Watkin appeals.

SLW – *I hadn't played in the one-day games for a few weeks. I could fully understand this as we were looking to the future and giving chances to others, but Sid had always said that I would play against Middlesex. I also played in the preceding Championship match against Surrey, and with a few showers forecast for the Sunday, I couldn't help thinking each time I finished a spell whether or not that would be my last ball for Glamorgan.*

My final over in the Middlesex match was a very emotional one, and I couldn't quite believe it that everyone was standing up applauding me when I was at the end of run-up for the final over. The applause built up with every ball, and then what was supposed to be my final ball was called a wide, and I had another delivery. It struck one of the tailenders on the pads, and I felt it was quite a good shout, but the umpire turned down my appeal.

Watkin then walked off to a standing ovation and there were handshakes all round to mark his outstanding contribution to Glamorgan cricket. The team then gathered on their dressing-room balcony at Sophia Gardens and the champagne corks were flying again as Steve James and his team were formally crowned as winners of Division Two of the Norwich Union League. The celebrations went on for many hours at the end of a day that had seen Glamorgan become the first county to go up in one competition and down in another.

Tragically, this was also the final game for another vital member of Glamorgan's set up – their loyal and popular scorer Byron Denning, who died six weeks later after a short illness. 'Dasher' had become part and parcel of the side, and although he always remained totally impartial in the scorebox, he took great pride and satisfaction in being part of one the most successful Glamorgan teams on record. He had become the club's scorer in 1983 after taking early retirement from the world of adult education, and during his time in office, he had logged the Sunday League win, the final of the Benson & Hedges Cup, as well as the County Championship title in 1997. This had really delighted Byron, and there were tears of sheer joy flowing down his happy face as he joined the rest of the team in the dressing room after they had won the title at Taunton.

During his time as Glamorgan's scorer, Byron's smiling face had become one of the most familiar and reassuring sights on Glamorgan's grounds whilst his voice was heard over the public address system, as he doubled up as the match-day announcer. Byron's gentle and mischievous humour over the tannoy enlightened many a dull day. Indeed, it was he, as befitted a proud grandfather, who at Abergavenny once told the ladies in the crowd to put their hands over the ears of any small children, in case they were distressed as he read out Glamorgan's bowling figures after they had been on the receiving end of a mauling by the visiting Worcestershire batsmen.

Another gem took place at Pentyrch in 1993, when Glamorgan visited the small club ground north of Cardiff, for the first and only time. The ground, set in open country-side, had virtually no distinguishing features apart from a small pavilion, but Dasher was

Farewell Watty.

The ever-genial Byron Denning, presenting an award to Tony Cottey at Cardiff.

in his element as on the horizon he could just about spy the Severn Estuary, some ten miles away, and the southern end was duly christened 'The Sea End'!

There was also the announcement at the end of a game at Pontypridd, after Hampshire had romped home early, thanks to a fierce spell of bowling from Malcolm Marshall, when Byron dryly told all and sundry that 'any spectators feeling entitled to a refund should write to Mr M.D. Marshall, c/o Hampshire CCC'. The match against Kent was also memorable, when Byron welcomed visiting officials and players to Cardiff, after their long motorway journey from the south-east and over the Severn Bridge, and then thanked them for their contributions towards the cost of the Second Severn Crossing!

SPJ – Byron was part of the furniture at the club – a brilliant bloke and a great friend of the players. He would never get involved on the technical side – but would always have a kind word for a player if they had played well, and would never say anything if you had done badly. Byron knew exactly how to approach each situation and he was always someone you looked forward to seeing on away trips in the team hotel or at the ground.

MPM – 'Dasher' had a great affinity with the players and we never thought of him as being an ex-committee man. Instead he was one of the boys, and in truth, he was our 13th man.

Glamorgan in the Norwich Union League – Division Two: 2001

29 April at Derby
Glamorgan 138 in 44.4 overs (K. Newell 47*, G. Welch 5-23)
Derbyshire 140-6 in 41.4 overs (D.G. Cork 83*, D.A. Cosker 2-21)
Derbyshire won by 4 wickets

20 May at Old Trafford
Lancashire 147-6 in 45 overs (N.H. Fairbrother 62, A.G. Wharf 3-23)
Glamorgan 148-6 in 40.5 overs (M.P. Maynard 39*, J. Wood 2-29)
Glamorgan won by 4 wickets

3 June at Swansea
Sussex 224-4 in 45 overs (R.R. Montgomerie 68, C.J. Adams 61*, A. Dale 2-29)
Glamorgan 228-4 in 42 overs (J.P. Maher 71, S.P. James 52*)
Glamorgan won by 6 wickets

10 June at Chelmsford
Essex 243-6 in 34 overs (R.C. Irani 108*, A. Dale 2-42)
Glamorgan 254-2 in 31.5 overs (K. Newell 97, M.P. Maynard 87*)
Glamorgan won by 8 wickets (D/L Method)

24 June at Sophia Gardens, Cardiff
Glamorgan 305-6 in 45 overs (J.P. Maher 94, R.D.B. Croft 59, A. Dale 52*)
Worcestershire 194 in 34.3 overs (D.A. Leatherdale 40, R.D.B. Croft 3-31)
Glamorgan won by 111 runs

8 July at Chester-le-Street
Glamorgan 145 in 40.2 overs (R.D.B. Croft 67, P.D. Collingwood 3-21)
Durham 146-8 in 43.3 overs (J.J.B. Lewis 46*, O.T. Parkin 2-24)
Durham won by 2 wickets

22 July at Sophia Gardens, Cardiff
Derbyshire 199-8 in 45 overs (S.D. Stubbings 60, M.P. Dowman 64, D.A. Cosker 3-40)
Glamorgan 200-4 in 40.4 overs (K. Newell 59, I.J. Thomas 53)
Glamorgan won by 6 wickets

5 August at Colwyn Bay
Glamorgan 266 in 43.5 overs (R.D.B. Croft 64, A. Flintoff 2-31)
Lancashire 220 in 41.5 overs (G.D. Lloyd 51, D.A. Cosker 3-58)
Glamorgan won by 46 runs

12 August at Southampton
Hampshire 120 in 38.5 overs (A.P. Davies 4-18, O.T. Parkin 3-39, A. Dale 3-22)
Glamorgan 121-4 in 27.5 overs (M.P. Maynard 41, A.D. Mullally 2-31)
Glamorgan won by 6 wickets

19 August at Sophia Gardens, Cardiff
Glamorgan 289-6 in 41 overs (K. Newell 65, R.D.B. Croft 92)
Essex 111 in 24.2 overs (A.P. Davies 5-39, R.D.B. Croft 2-12)
Glamorgan won by 178 runs

26 August at Lord's
Glamorgan 100-3 in 21 overs v. Middlesex
No result

27 August at Sophia Gardens, Cardiff
Glamorgan 250-9 in 45 overs (M.P. Maynard 54, S.J. Harmison 4-43)
Durham 226 in 44 overs (N. Peng 92, O.T. Parkin 3-37, S.D. Thomas 3-27)
Glamorgan won by 24 runs

29 August at Sophia Gardens, Cardiff (Day-night)
Glamorgan 244-6 in 45 overs (M.P. Maynard 116*, A.D. Mascarenhas 2-37)
Hampshire 193 in 40.2 overs (N.C. Johnson 66, R.D.B. Croft 4-33)
Glamorgan won by 51 runs

2 September at Worcester
Glamorgan 254-6 in 43 overs (R.D.B. Croft 61, M.P. Maynard 71) v. Worcestershire
No Result

4 September at Hove (Day-night)
Sussex 225-2 in 45 overs (C.J. Adams 100*, M.W. Goodwin 67*)
Glamorgan 191 in 42.5 overs (J.P. Maher 54, B.V. Taylor 3-43)
Sussex won by 34 runs

16 September at Sophia Gardens, Cardiff
Glamorgan 272-4 in 45 overs (R.D.B. Croft 114, S.P. James 93, C.B. Keegan 3-42)
Middlesex 232-8 in 45 overs (S.J. Cook 50, A.P. Davies 3-36, A. Dale 2-33)
Glamorgan won by 40 runs

13

More Canterbury Tales

One of the principles behind the ECB's decision to split both the Championship and one-day League into two divisions was to make the county game more competitive. Many traditionalists disagreed with their suggestions, whilst others felt that other things could be done in order to 'raise the standard'. But two divisions came in, and in 2002 Glamorgan carved their own unique place in English cricket history by becoming the first county side to win Division One of the National League the year after being winners of Division Two – a record that can never be beaten, but only equalled, and one that was set up in 2001 by eight wins at home, followed in 2002 by a clean sweep away from home.

Their success in 2002 culminated in a cliffhanger of a match against Kent, and as the celebrations began on the pavilion at the St Lawrence Ground, many comparisons were made with Glamorgan's 1993 pilgrimage to Canterbury. But there were important differences with their previous one-day title, and in fact, there were closer comparisons with their Championship success in 1997 as the club had opted for an overseas bowler rather than a batsman, as in 1993.

Despite the success of Jimmy Maher in 2001 and Matthew Elliott the previous summer, the club felt that an experienced international bowler was essential so that someone could step into the boots vacated by Steve Watkin. Many names were bandied around, including Pakistani pace ace Wasim Akram, but the final choice was Michael Kasprowicz, the thirty-year-old seam bowler from Queensland who had a fine record in both Tests and One-Day Internationals for Australia, and who had been the leading wicket-taker in domestic cricket in Australia during the 2001/02 season.

'Kasper' soon made his presence felt and in Glamorgan's opening National League game at Cardiff against the Durham Dynamos, the Australian produced a lively opening spell of 3 for 18 in seven overs to put the visitors on the back foot as they chased a target of 162. The two spinners, Croft and Cosker, then maintained the stranglehold, with their combined 18 overs yielding only three boundaries, and the Dragons opened their account with a 20-run victory.

However, the wily Kasprowicz could not transform Glamorgan's form in the Benson & Hedges Cup, and for the second successive summer, the Welsh county enjoyed a sorry season in the competition, losing all their matches as well as Matthew Maynard, who broke his hand after being struck by Mark Alleyne in the match with Gloucestershire. Glamorgan also made a poor start in their first Championship encounter, losing to Derbyshire at Cardiff by 163 runs.

But Kasper then came good at Worcester as Glamorgan defeated the New Road club by 110 runs, with the Australian taking 5-77 in a wholehearted display of seam bowling,

Michael Kasprowicz.

wheeling away for over two hours unchanged. Then in the next match against Durham at Cardiff, Darren Thomas took centre stage by taking ten wickets as Glamorgan recorded a five-wicket win to lift the County into early contention for promotion from Division Two of the Championship.

Early season wins over Durham and Leicestershire in the Norwich Union League also meant that the Dragons were riding high in the one-day league, although the nature of the fixture list meant that they had only played three games by the end of June. But by this time, the County were still unbeaten and had their morale lifted by a thrilling tie against Kent at Cardiff. Early morning rain meant that the match was reduced to a 23-overs-a-side contest, and Glamorgan were given a rapid start by a breezy start by opener Robert Croft and the left-hander David Hemp, who had returned to Glamorgan from Warwickshire at the start of the season.

Their efforts meant that Kent needed 155 at a rate of 6.7 and after a half-century in even time from Robert Key, the visitors looked the more likely winners at the start of the final over, needing 6 runs to win with 4 wickets intact. But after failing to score from Adrian Dale's first delivery, Geraint Jones was caught off the next, and when Mark Ealham was out to the fourth, Kent still needed six runs to win. James Golding struck the fifth ball for a boundary, but could only scramble a single from the final delivery to leave the game tied.

AD – *I think Sid didn't really intend me to have a bowl that day, but he had to throw me the ball after getting the bowling changes a bit mixed up. I don't think he went to Cambridge for his maths!*

The final two weeks of June were perhaps the defining period of the summer and three very different and truly remarkable games highlighted the spirit and self-belief of the Glamorgan players. Firstly, on 19 June they were involved in one of the most amazing one-day games ever in the fourth round of the Cheltenham and Gloucester Trophy against Surrey at The Oval.

With Steve James back in Cardiff to be at the bedside of his daughter who had been rushed into hospital, Robert Croft took over the captaincy, but he lost the toss, and the home side batted first. Thanks to Ali Brown, Surrey proceeded to re-write the one-day record books with an astonishing 438-5 as Brown made 268. Both were world records

– for the highest-ever team total, and the highest-ever individual innings – with Brown striking 30 fours and 12 sixes in his record-breaking knock.

RDBC – *I don't think anyone will ever again see such a display of clean hitting as Alistair Brown gave. It was phenomenal. We had some early chances, but we didn't take them. When we gathered in the dressing room afterwards, I told the boys to show passion and pride, and basically I told them to just go out there and smash it. They did that and I was so proud of every one of the players.*

The acting captain led from the front, hitting a blistering 119 as he reached his hundred off just 56 balls. For most of their innings, Glamorgan were ahead of where Surrey had been at the same stage, as David Hemp made 102, whilst Darren Thomas hit a quick-fire 71 off just 41 balls. But in the end, their sterling efforts were not quite enough as Surrey ended up victors by 9 runs in an amazing game that had produced 867 runs – another world record.

SDT – *Ali Brown's innings was magnificent. He was in the zone and he played intelligently. He seemed to start every over I bowled to him by hitting the first ball through extra cover. Then when I dragged my length back, he would go back and play a pull or pick-up shot to the short leg-side boundary. The game was something of a freak show. Every bowler was punished. We were lucky to have enough balls to complete the match, and it seemed that one ball would be coming from outside the ground just as another was going out – but at least we let them know they were in a game. Browny said afterwards that the fifty overs he spent in the field were the most frightening of his life. He just didn't expect to have the worst fifty overs in the field after spending the best fifty overs of his career at the crease.*

Alistair Brown celebrates at The Oval during his remarkable innings. (Image © EMPICS Sports Photo Agency.)

'Just go out there and smash it.' Robert Croft's words of advice at The Oval in 2002.

Opposite page: Matthew Maynard batting against Warwickshire.

DAC – *That was the most bizarre, unrealistic one-day game that I have ever been involved in. A short boundary on one side and a flat wicket – I felt at times when we bowling that we would have had more success and movement bowling on the nearby M25! In some ways, I got off a little light only going for 57 in seven overs. Any other team chasing above 400 in a 50-over game, you would have written off straight away. But not Glamorgan – the harder the challenge, the more ridiculously outrageous we became. Crofty set the tone hitting the first five balls for four, and at the end of the day we just fell short. Another great day, and one that was like a springboard for our remaining games! No target seemed too much and we were very confident of defending any total, especially away from home.*

IJT – *It was possibly the one-day game of the century – at least that's how I will describe it to my grandchildren! The fielding was not needed as it mainly went through the gaps or out of the ground. I really did feel for Crofty at that time – how do you set a field to a batsman who was being so destructive? My real memory was fielding in the covers – we had an extra cover, cover, wide mid-off, and a deep cover, but still Ali Brown hit the ball over and through the covers to the boundary rope.*

The team talk before going out was quite simple – Crofty simply said let's smash it, and then went straight out to hit 5 fours in the first over. I was standing at the non-striker's end, and that first over was a joy to watch. The look on Martin Bicknell's face as his fourth delivery was despatched to the boundary just said it all – he just laughed, and gave a shrug of the shoulders as wherever he put it, Crofty got hold of it and smashed it.

APD – *This is one game I will never forget but, walking off at the mid-way point, I felt exactly the opposite. The innings that Ali Brown played that day was something that*

very few people in the world can do. He is one of the cleanest hitters of a ball I have seen and nothing that he did that day proved otherwise. Walking out to bowl, I recall Darren turning to me and saying no worries, in two and a half hours time it will all be over and we'll be watching our boys knock the runs off. If only it could have been that easy! It was like circus balls were disappearing here there and everywhere. You simply couldn't bowl anywhere to him. The fun part came when we batted and I think it transformed our season and made a lot of other teams sit up and look at us. Crofty, Hempy, Matt, Daley and Thommo all played like gods and if it wasn't for two great overs by Giddins at the end, then I'm sure we would have clinched a historic victory.

MPM *– That incredible game was probably the defining moment of the summer. We went so desperately close to beating them, but it gave us tremendous confidence,*

Adrian Dale.

The Wales team congratulate Robert Croft after the off-spinner takes a wicket against England in the one-day 'international' against England.

because we knew from then, that we could chase virtually anything, and on another day, we might even have won that game.

Five days later, the majority of the Glamorgan squad were involved in a ground-breaking 'home international' at Sophia Gardens as the England one-day side played a Wales team as part of their warm-up for the triangular tournament with India and Sri Lanka. Somerset's Steffan Jones, Sussex's Tony Cottey and South African Jacques Kallis joined the bulk of the Glamorgan squad for the 50-over friendly with the English side. The match may have been 'friendly' in name, but Steve James' Welsh side were eager to beat the English team, and this was evident as a fired-up performance in the field restricted the English side to 189 for 9 after they had been put in.

SPJ – All of the boys were really focused for that game, whilst on a personal level I was just so happy to be back playing. Bethan had been very ill in hospital and then I'd picked up a nasty stomach bug. In fact, I turned up the day before the game hoping to have a net, but I was sick and had to return home feeling quite rough. Luckily, I was OK on the Monday morning and it was great to get back into action, especially knowing that Bethan was on the mend. I felt very relaxed in the field and always felt we were in control as England never really got to terms with the Cardiff wicket.

Right from the start of the match Wales were the superior team, as firstly Jacques Kallis and Andrew Davies bowled accurate opening spells, before Steffan Jones and Darren Thomas ripped the heart out of the English middle order as three wickets fell for 16 runs in a nine-over spell from the two Welshmen. Robert Croft then delivered an exemplary spell of off-spin as the English lower order tried to step up the run-rate, but the damage had already been done.

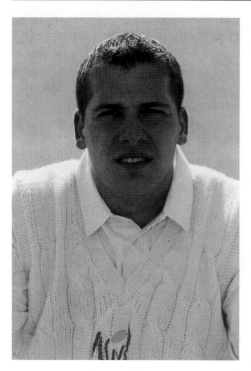

Ian Thomas.

The English bowlers were then put to the sword as Robert Croft gave his side a flying start with Matthew Hoggard bowling eight wides and two no balls in a seven-over spell which yielded 63 runs, before Steve James and David Hemp shared a partnership of 132 for the second wicket as the Welsh side strolled to an eight-wicket win.

The following weekend the Glamorgan side were in National League action at Taunton in what was viewed by the Somerset supporters as a rather controversial game played in cloudy and showery weather. There were a couple of interruptions as Somerset batted first and made a poor start against a hostile salvo of swing bowling from Andrew Davies, who took 3 for 20 in his opening spell. Their middle order subsequently initiated a recovery and Somerset passed the 200 mark, before further interruptions saw Glamorgan face a readjusted target.

Glamorgan slumped to 47 for 4, before Adrian Dale played a responsible innings of 63, and with rain in the air, all eyes were on the scoreboard at the end of each over to see who was ahead under the Duckworth-Lewis format. The position see-sawed from one side to the other, and with the rain seemingly about to end the game at any minute, Somerset slowed things down hoping to win on the Duckworth-Lewis. But the rain held off, and Glamorgan lost a series of quick wickets to put the home side back on top with Glamorgan needing twelve runs from Steffan Jones' final over with two wickets in hand.

But the cut-off time for the final over had been passed, so the two umpires awarded Glamorgan six penalty runs in light of Somerset's slow-over rate. The equation was now a more manageable six from six, and Kasper eased Celtic nerves with a four and a single before Andrew Davies scampered the winning runs off the penultimate ball.

Glamorgan's momentum up the National League was temporarily halted the following weekend at Swansea, as they slumped to a five-wicket defeat – their first at home in the competition since the end of the 2000 season. But they got back into winning ways in mid-July at Trent Bridge as they comprehensively defeated Nottinghamshire by 8 wickets, and then travelled to the Cheltenham Festival for the Championship encounter with Gloucestershire, where Matthew Maynard produced another vintage display of batsmanship as Glamorgan won a superb game of cricket by two wickets.

On his previous visit to the Cheltenham ground in 1991, Maynard had struck a century in each innings of the match, and he repeated his feat with scores of 140 and 118*, oozing class and a cool temperament as well after Glamorgan had been set a target of 317 to win on the final day. The wicket was also starting to assist the spin bowlers, but Maynard, drawing on all of his experience, quietly played himself in, picked off the singles and then started to pepper the boundary boards again.

MPM – *It was a good cricket wicket – a bit in it for the seamers and there was something there for the spinners too. It was a very special game for me as I passed 20,000 runs for Glamorgan, and recorded my 50th first-class hundred. Cheltenham will therefore always hold very special memories for me.*

However, wickets started to fall at the other end, and it forced Michael Kasprowicz, one of the walking wounded in the Glamorgan side, to don his pads and come out to bat. Kasper had pulled a hamstring whilst bowling, so when he came out to bat, Dan Cherry, the young opening batsman, re-appeared as his runner.

DDC – *I was a bit nervous and pumped up, and I certainly didn't want to get involved in an awful muddle and get Matthew run out. Despite the run-chase and fall of wickets, Matthew was so very calm, almost as if he was in the nets. Watching him bat was a real privilege and I think his hundred in the second innings was the best of its kind that I have seen as a team member. It was a great feeling when we won the*

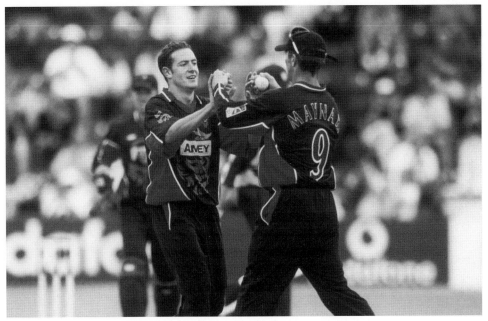

Dean Cosker is congratulated by Matthew Maynard after the left-arm spinner claims a vital wicket.

David Hemp.

game, especially when Simon Jones came in and finished it with a six and a four into the tents around the boundary edge. When I had returned to the dressing rooms when Kasper was out, Simon had said to Steve James, 'Put me in now and the game will be over half an hour earlier.' He didn't put him in then, but I'm sure Simon's self confidence would have made him finish the game if he had!

To break into the first team was a brilliant experience for me. Not only was I playing for Glamorgan, but I was playing in the same team as some of my boyhood heroes. I was only thirteen when we won the Sunday League in 1993, so to play with people such as Matt, Daley, Crofty and Jamer who were a part of that fine team, was great. To play with, and watch these guys in action, was what I had always wanted to do as a kid when I started playing in Pembrokeshire.

The best thing for me going into the side was being able to open the batting with Jamer. He is the ultimate pro and he works so hard. It was brilliant to go out to bat with him, knowing that he was at the other end even if we did not share a big part-nership. His innings at Chelmsford was awesome for the powers of concentration that he showed – one ball at a time, and he never looked like getting out.

James' 249 in the Championship match against Essex was the sixth time he had posted a double-century for the club, and it was the highest-ever innings by a visiting batsman at Chelmsford, beating Wally Hammond's 244 for Gloucestershire in 1928. The Glamorgan captain also helped his side rattle up the small matter of 499 runs on the second day of the match with Essex – the most they had ever scored in a day's play in their entire history.

But after his fantastic innings, Steve James' knee swelled up and prevented him from playing in the following Norwich Union match at Edgbaston. However, this gave Ian

Matt and
Deano the
Dragon!

Mike Powell.

Thomas a chance to display his talents at the top of the order, and he blasted a career-best 72 against a lacklustre and wayward Warwickshire attack. Together with half-centuries from Adrian Dale and Matthew Maynard, Thomas saw Glamorgan to a mammoth 300-8, and all after having spent the previous day and a half in the field at Chelmsford. But the Warwickshire batsmen showed less resistance against the Glamorgan attack than the Essex batsmen had done the previous day, and the Dragons stormed to a 62-run victory.

IJT – *I didn't really know that I was playing until half an hour before the start, but it turned out to be a good day for me as I recorded my one-day personal best, and it was great being out there – we fielded extremely well on what was a hot afternoon, and the Glammy following was brilliant, competing for noise with the Bears fans. The bowling spells from Alex Wharf and Owen Parkin set the tone, before the spin twins Croft and Cosker came on to once again work their magic This was another fine all-round team performance and to play like that on a Test ground, and against a good one-day team, all helped to build up our confidence for later in the season.*

The first weekend of August saw Glamorgan involved in back-to-back League games with the Somerset Sabres at Cardiff and then away to the Worcestershire Royals. Both were hit by rain, with Somerset winning the first match, but the following day, it was the Dragons who finished on top and secured a decisive victory over the Worcestershire side who were also pressing for the League title. They seemed to be having the better of things as the Royals posted a decent score of 202-9, and then in reply Glamorgan slumped to 28-3.

But the following half a dozen overs saw Steve James and Matthew Maynard turn the game on its head as they punished a rather wayward three-over spell from Shane Lee, Worcestershire's replacement overseas player, who had not played for several months following a knee operation. The Australian failed to find his radar with the ball, and in the space of a handful of overs, Glamorgan had galloped on to 108 for 3. More importantly, they were ahead under the Duckworth-Lewis system, so as light rain turned into a thunderstorm, the Dragons were able to celebrate another precious victory.

They maintained their quest for the title by beating Yorkshire at Cardiff, thanks to an opening stand of 84 in 13.5 overs by Robert Croft and Ian Thomas, followed by a career-best spell of 4-17. Then under the Durham floodlights, Steve James played an invaluable captain's innings as the Dragons turned the formbook upside down by successfully chasing a target of 162 under the lights and on a wicket of variable bounce.

The captain followed this up with an undefeated half-century in the League game at Colwyn Bay, easily his favourite ground, and against Nottinghamshire, whose bowlers must have been as sick to death of seeing his bat by the end of their visit to North Wales as in the Championship match; 'Sid' scored 184 – his eighth first-class century against them. When he was stumped, it brought to an end an astonishing sequence that had seen James score 752 runs at the ground without being dismissed.

During the Championship game at Rhos-on-Sea, Michael Kasprowicz had to leave the field with sore shins. The medical advice was that he should have a scan in hospital. Fortunately, it showed no permanent damage to his lower leg, but what it did reveal was that the lion-hearted Aussie had a fractured bone in his foot. Remarkably, the injury had been sustained back in May, when Kasper was struck on the foot by fellow Queenslander Andy Bichel, during the match against Worcestershire.

Whilst Kasper had continued to bowl since being struck by Bichel, he was unable to play in the next Norwich Union League match at Headingley against Yorkshire, who two days before had won the NatWest Trophy at Lord's. Then on the morning of the match at Leeds, the Dragons also lost Darren Thomas with a back spasm, and it looked as if injuries were going to hit the Welsh county at the most vital time of the season. But up stepped young all-rounder David Harrison, and despite having never taken a wicket before in the competition, the

David Harrison.

Robert Croft – Glamorgan's captain for the Canterbury match in 2002.

twenty-one-year-old seamer took 5 for 26 at the Leeds ground as Yorkshire were bustled out for 167. Then after Robert Croft and Ian Thomas had once again struck brisk fifties, Harrison came in at number 3 to hit an unbeaten 37 and put the finishing touches to a comprehensive nine-wicket win that further extended the Dragon's lead at the top of the table.

DSH – *I had started really well in the second team, and was quiet hopeful of getting a chance in the first team. Returning to India in February, where I worked with Dennis Lillee helped me a great deal. I felt a different bowler and a different person. It was good as well to work with Steve Watkin, and if there was anything I needed, he was there. I don't think there is a better man in the country to help seam bowlers.*

But then in early July whilst playing in a Second-XI fixture at Usk, I picked up a side injury. It felt as if somebody had shot me in my side. I thought that was it for the season, and felt my chance of playing first-team cricket in the year 2002 was gone. Three weeks later my luck changed as I played against Worcestershire in a League game, and bowled a tidy spell. Then when I was back playing in club cricket, my phone rang. 'Dave, it's John Derrick here. Can you come up to Headingley tonight as cover for Darren Thomas.

So off I went to Headingley, and then the next morning, Darren had to pull out of the game. I really felt for him, because he had done really well for the team and he is someone who has helped me a lot over the years and I have a lot of respect for him. Steve James then told me that I would be playing, and nerves kicked in straight away. I get really nervous before most games but this was a huge game for the club.

I settled down a bit having bowled a maiden in my first over to Craig White. From then on, I felt quiet comfortable, and was lucky enough to pick up a few wickets. Then to go in at three with the bat was a complete shock. I was sent in to pinch hit, so I just went in and tried to enjoy myself! I was really pleased the way the day went as a whole, and having worked hard in the second team earlier in the year, my wickets and runs gave me great satisfaction. But more importantly, it was a win for the club that took us top of the table.

With three games remaining, including a game at Canterbury, there was plenty of talk in the media about Glamorgan repeating their pilgrimage down to Kent in 1993 and winning the League title. Several articles were written recalling the feats of the Glamorgan team nine years before, but the 2002 team was a different one to that in 1993. As the match at Headingley had shown, the Dragons were frequently being given a rapid start by pinch-hitter Robert Croft and young tyro Ian Thomas, rather than the regular opening batsmen. Their seam bowlers were also more intent on attack than on containment, with Andrew Davies, and Michael Kasprowicz regularly amongst the wickets.

MPM – *In 2002 we were attack-minded – hunting for wickets with the ball, and geared up to attack from the off with the bat. We had more of a strike force with the bowlers, and if there was the odd four-ball, we would shrug that off because we were looking for wickets. Back in 1993, we had a coaching consultant plan out our*

Mike Powell – the scorer of vital runs in the floodlit match against Worcestershire.

strategy before the start of the season. We were set fixed boundaries, like when we were bowling, the intention was that the opposition were not to have scored more than 30 after ten overs. Conversely when we batted, we wanted to keep wickets in hand. That was the priority and if we made less than 30 after ten, we'd have been pretty content so long as we hadn't lost wickets. In 2002 we had aggressive batsmen like Ian Thomas and Crofty at the top of the order, so again it was onto the attack right from the start.

But there were some common elements – the accurate and penetrative off-spin of Robert Croft, the fine catching, plus the superb batting talents of Matthew Maynard. The thirty-six year old rolled back the years with a scintillating display of batting in the Dragon's next match – the day-night encounter with their nearest rivals, the Worcestershire Royals at Cardiff.

Both teams knew the importance of this game, and a capacity crowd thronged into the Sophia Gardens to watch the encounter that in effect would decide the outcome of the Division One title. The Royals made the better start as the Dragons slumped to 24 for 2, but then Mike Powell and Matthew Maynard revived memories of their efforts in the 2000 season, sharing a stand of 133 in 19 overs. This time it was Powell who was the more assertive early on, with the twenty-five year old unleashing some powerful drives as Maynard quietly pushed the ball around.

MJP – *I just went out and tried to play in as positive a way as possible. Although there was a massive crowd, I didn't try to build it up in my mind. J.D.'s words were to just play normally and stick to my game plan. He said not to panic and the runs would eventually come. He was absolutely right – they did. He's been a big mastermind behind everything over the past few years, and I have a lot to thank J.D. for.*

MPM – *Mike really showed what he could do batting at number 3. He's not a nurdler and is more of a strong hitter. He really got us going that day, and helped us post a really great total. In fact we had so many runs on the board that even if Hick had scored a hundred, Worcestershire might not have even won.*

After Powell had gone for an impressive 71, Maynard took the attack to the Worcestershire bowlers, and he was in sight of his second successive century in floodlit games at Cardiff when he gave Gareth Batty a return catch, and departed for 87. Maynard's awesome innings really gave his side a spur, and Worcestershire never looked like scoring the 281 runs they needed against an accurate attack, including Michael Kasprowicz, who played through the pain barrier after a cortisone injection before the game.

The brave Australian was also supported by some outstanding ground fielding and catching, with Dean Cosker excelling, as he had done all season, just backward of square on the offside. When Graeme Hick and Ben Smith were dismissed in the space of four runs, Worcestershire had slumped to 91 for 5, and despite some lusty swings from David Leatherdale, the Worcestershire innings quickly folded, with the last three wickets falling in successive balls.

DSH – *The ground was jam-packed and there was a great atmosphere. Again, I was lucky to start with a maiden when I started bowling, and then after taking the wicket of Graeme Hick, walking back to my fielding spot was a moment I'll never forget. People were standing up, clapping and chanting my name! It was like I was dreaming, and I didn't want the game to stop! After we had won, I thought I was on top of the world, but then in the early hours of the next morning, I woke up with a severe pain in my stomach. I was screaming and shouting with pain, so Mark Wallace, my house-mate, drove me to hospital where acute food poisoning was diagnosed, and I stayed there the next day – what a 24 hours!'*

The demolition of Worcestershire meant that a win, or two points, on 15 September against Kent at Canterbury would guarantee the Welsh county the First Division title. As in 1993, there was an exodus of Welsh sporting fans down to the St Lawrence ground, and on the coaches, mini-buses and trains, the County's supporters nervously chattered away about what hopefully would happen, and whether the 1993 side was better than the 2002 one.

They were treated to a wonderful and dramatic game of cricket, the script of which even Geoffrey Chaucer would have been hard pressed to match, but for all of the Dragon's supporters who had made the long journey down to Canterbury, what mattered most was that at the end of the day, the character and fortitude of the Welsh side showed through as they won the title. Their collective spirit and belief in themselves helped them to hold their composure just when it mattered most, and paid Viv Richards back for the vital lessons he had taught the senior members of the side back in the early 1990s. There was though, one senior member of the Dragons side missing, as Steve James had broken a finger in the match against Worcestershire, and it was Robert Croft, his able deputy, who won an important toss and elected to bat first.

Once again, the backbone of the Dragons innings was provided by Mike Powell whose composed innings of 74 from 83 balls set Glamorgan on course for a decent score. However, there were a few stutters en route, and they only reached 226 for 7 thanks to a level-headed innings of 43 by Adrian Dale, supported by an aggressive cameo of 37 off 31 balls from David Hemp, who had been restored to the side in James' absence.

The pressure on the Glamorgan side rose even more as news came in from Trent Bridge that Worcestershire were well on top of Nottinghamshire and poised to narrow the gap at the top of the table. Glamorgan therefore had to win at Canterbury to prevent the game going down to the wire the following week at Cardiff, but the target of 227 was within the home team's grasp. Their batsmen also had an extra reason for wanting to do well, as it was Matthew Fleming's final game at Canterbury and they wanted to give him the perfect send-off with a successful run-chase.

Despite a teatime presentation and a fly-past from a Spitfire bomber, it was not to be a fairytale end to Fleming's career as he was caught by David Hemp in the third over. The pressure on the Kent batsmen was maintained by some lively Glamorgan fielding, backed up by some astute bowling changes by Robert Croft. In particular, Croft introduced David Harrison into the attack in the tenth over, and with his fifth delivery, he dismissed Rob Key. Croft also switched Andrew Davies to the Pavilion End where, with the final ball of his first over at the Pavilion End, he claimed the prized scalp of the Australian Steve Waugh.

However, Mark Ealham still posed a threat and with the support of Matthew Walker, they took Kent closer to their target. But their rate of progress was slowed by the accurate spin of Croft and Cosker, and it was Croft who dismissed both batsmen with his subtle variations, including balls delivered at least a couple of yards from behind the popping crease.

But even then Kent did not give up the fight, and Paul Nixon, their jaunty wicket-keeper, then led a lower-order rally with rookie batsman Geraint Jones. Mike Powell took a stunning catch on the boundary to dismiss Jones, but this brought in another youngster, Alex Loudon, who was equally determined to continue the run-chase. Together with Nixon, the pair reduced the equation to fifteen off the last twelve balls with four wickets in hand, but Andrew Davies then held his nerve to deliver a fine over during which he dismissed Loudon and Martin Saggers in successive deliveries, all of which left Kent still needing ten from the final over of the game.

Up stepped Michael Kasprowicz to bowl what were for Glamorgan the most important six balls for many years. Off the first, Nixon edged the ball past the outstretched gloves of Mark Wallace, and the ball sped down to the third-man boundary. It looked like being a decisive stroke, but Adrian Dale ran around, picked up the ball, and sent an arrow-like

THE *RUN OUT*

The Glamorgan team celebrate after winning the Norwich Union title at Canterbury.

return back to the 'keeper as Nixon came back for a second run. The diving Wallace then whipped off the bails to beat a desperate lunge by Nixon, and after confirmation from the third umpire, the Kent man was run out.

AD – I was down there on the third-man boundary, knowing that there was a good chance of the ball coming my way as Kasper planned to bowl yorkers outside Nixon's off-stump. I had been struggling to throw all summer so when the ball came to me, I gathered it up as quick as I could, but becuase of my damaged shoulder my return was a bit short of the target. But Mark Wallace had got into a great position, and whipped off the bails. To be honest, we weren't sure whether or not Nixon was out, and as the third umpire deliberated, we gathered around Kasper to plan the rest of the over. It was a fantastic feeling when Nixon was confirmed as being out.

Kasper and the rest of the Glamorgan fielders then held their nerve, as James Tredwell and Ben Trott could only scamper three singles, plus a leg bye, and when Trott – ironically the man who Cosker had dismissed at Taunton in 1997 when Glamorgan won the Championship – swung at and missed Kasprowicz's final delivery, the Dragons had secured a four-run victory to win the Division One title and the cheque for £54,000. As at Canterbury in 1993 and at Taunton in 1997, the celebrations went on long into the night, and for Mike Powell, who had been Glamorgan's top-scorer earlier in the afternoon, the champagne tasted even sweeter.

NORWICH UNION
LEAGUE

NORWICH UNION LEAGUE
DIVISION ONE CHAMPIONS
2002

NORWICH UNION
LEAGUE

The celebrations continue at Cardiff at the end of the 2002 season.

MJP – *I had played in a few games back in 1997, but I wasn't actually at Taunton for the final game when the Championship was won. It was great to have played a bigger part this time, and to enjoy all the celebrations in the dressing room. It was brilliant to be part of it and to score a few runs in such an important game was simply superb. It was also my first-ever Man of the Match award, and I was so proud to receive the award at the end of the game. The senior lads had been through it all before, but it was fantastic for the likes of myself and Andrew Davies, who I've been playing cricket with since I was fourteen, and Mark Wallace, who I grew up with in the same village. At the end of the match, Wally and I ran up and hugged each other. We've been playing together since our school days in Crickhowell and it was great to share a proud moment like that.*

A lot of other teams admire us for this togetherness, and our desire to play for each other. Apart from Kasper, we had all come up together through the Welsh Schools system, and as we have all grown up together, the youngsters don't feel under pressure. After the presentation ceremony had finished, Kasper sat us all down in the dressing room and got everyone to say a few words about what winning the League meant to them. It was very emotional to hear everyone say their bit. None of it had been scripted beforehand, and we all spoke from the heart. It's what they do in Queensland, and for me that day at Canterbury is what all those long hours of training are about. When I'm out in the winter, running up and down the hills in the pouring rain, I'll think about that wonderful day in Kent.

SPJ – *It was probably the most nerve-racking afternoon of my life; being sat up there on the balcony, not being able to do anything at all about what was going on out there on the pitch. I never want to be a spectator in that kind of situation again! I was always confident that we would win, and I was gutted not to be out there when we did.*

I felt throughout the length of the match that, given time, we'd come through, and so it proved. That's what happened throughout the season. When the pressure was on, the boys have stuck their hands up and taken responsibility and done the job. We picked ourselves up after a poor start to the one-day season and got our act together. I think we thoroughly deserved to win the trophy at Canterbury.

RDBC – *The win took on a bit of a different meaning to the one at Canterbury in 1993. That year we had been the underdogs, whereas in 2002 we were the favourites, and that can sometimes be a little bit harder. There were obviously periods when we thought the victory was slipping away, and when they started hitting boundaries in the last ten overs or so, I started thinking that Kent were now the favourites to win. But to quote Jimmy Greaves, it's a funny old game, and we just had to stick by the good things we'd done all year. I was very proud of my players out there. There were sticky times, but as happened throughout the summer, at vital times people just chipped in and did their bit. Young and old – we all pulled together, and that's all you can ask for. It was for moments like that at Canterbury that you play the game.*

DSH – *The whole build-up to the game was a great experience, and it felt like being in a football cup final. On the day, you could sense the tension around the ground and in the dressing room. With a small boundary and so many Glamorgan supporters close to the action, it created a great atmosphere! Getting Robert Key out in the first over helped with the nerves, but I was nervous every time I started on my run-up. The last four overs of the game were absolutely frightening! I could feel myself shaking down at third man. When that final ball was bowled, I was the most relieved man in the world – having all that tension and nervousness leave your body and be replaced by emotion and joy was a feeling I will never ever forget.*

I sat in the dressing room after the game and spent a couple of minutes to myself, just to take everything in. I felt myself overcome with emotion, and there were tears rolling down my cheeks. This showed how much the whole club meant to me and told me that all the hard work that I had done earlier in the year had paid off. Later, Kasper sat us down in the dressing room after the game, and got all the boys to say a few words. That was a special moment, and something that I will never forget. For me, to be sat in a room with players that were my heroes as a young cricketer, and to have achieved something with them as players and friends was a dream come true.

APD – *It was a game where we didn't perform brilliantly, but did just enough. For me, my own individual highlight was getting the wicket of Steve Waugh, but this didn't hit home until well into the next day when I had had time to think about exactly what Glamorgan had achieved. However, getting that wicket would have meant nothing had the game gone the other way, as it quite easily could have done. Winning the League and being part of that changing room is something that no one can ever take from me and I will cherish those memories for the rest of my life. A changing room is a very sacred place, and late on when everyone had their individual say, it was clear that we have a changing room in which everyone respects one another. There are no superstars, just a squad of players all wanting to be successful for the Daffodil.*

MAW – *There are boards up in our dressing room in Cardiff with the names of the players from 1993 and 1997, and when I've looked up at them, it's shown me what the game is all about. Now we'll have another board put up, and I'll be able to look up at that and take a great deal of pride from having been involved.*

DLH – *I was twelfth man back in 1993, so it was just fantastic to get play at Canterbury this time, and then be part of a winning side. I got 37, but more importantly, it was great for the side to win. As an outsider coming into the team, I think the reason for our success in the League competition stemmed from the way all the players were so confident of getting results. I have to admit, I can't explain why it is that we were in such a positive frame of mind when playing in the coloured clothes and with the white ball. Why we didn't have that same sort of confidence and performance level in the Benson's at the start of the season is hard to explain.*

IJT – *I had been disappointed not to play in the first League game of the season against Durham, and I had sat in the crowd feeling a bit miffed. But it only encouraged me to be more determined in getting a place in the side, and little did I think at the time that I would win the League with that same team. It was an honour to be part of the side and the team meeting after the Kent game, before we left the ground to celebrate, was one of the most emotional I'd ever experienced in cricket. Everybody sat down to have a say about what winning the title meant to them and how they really felt about it. It showed the pride and honour the boys have in playing and winning for Glamorgan, and Wales! The emotions shown that day in Kent inspire you to want to repeat it and gain further success for the club and its loyal supporters.*

DDC – *I was twelfth man for a few of the one-day League games. It was quite nerve-racking for me, but watching from the side and in the dressing room there was always a sense that the boys could not be beaten. That was probably why we won the title – not only had the team got into the habit of winning from the year before, but we had a good mixture of youth and experience. I hope the youngsters who are coming through can carry on learning from the likes of Jamer, Matt and Crofty and bring even more success for the club.*

Glamorgan in the Norwich Union League – Division One: 2002

19 May at Sophia Gardens, Cardiff
Glamorgan 161-8 in 45 overs (M.J. Powell 47*, N. Killeen 3-29, A.M. Davies 2-24)
Durham 141-9 in 45 overs (A. Pratt 42, M.S. Kasprowicz 4-28, A.P. Davies 2-17,
  R.D.B. Croft 2-26)
Glamorgan won by 20 runs

4 June at Leicester
Glamorgan 194-6 in 45 overs (S.P. James 86, C.D. Crowe 2-34, M.J.A. Whiley 2-36)
Leicestershire 149 in 39.2 overs (I.J. Sutcliffe 57, A. Dale 3-28, R.D.B. Croft 2-17)
Glamorgan won by 45 runs

9 June at Sophia Gardens, Cardiff
Glamorgan 155-7 in 23 overs (D.L. Hemp 39, M.V. Fleming 2-24, J.C. Tredwell 2-23)
Kent 155-9 in 23 overs (R.W.T. Key 51, A. Dale 2-5, A.P. Davies 2-25)
Match Tied

30 June at Taunton
Somerset 220-9 in 45 overs (M. Burns 51, M.J. Wood 58, A.P. Davies 4-33,
  R.D.B. Croft 2-37)
Glamorgan 209-9 in 38.5 overs (A. Dale 63, P.S. Jones 3-36)
Glamorgan won by 1 wicket (D/L Method)

7 July at Swansea
Glamorgan 220-8 in 45 overs (P.A.J. De Freitas 4-24, C.D. Crowe 2-38, A.Dale 78*)
Leicestershire 221-5 in 44.2 overs (I.J. Sutcliffe 67, R.D.B. Croft 2-19)
Leicestershire won by 5 wickets

14 July at Trent Bridge
Nottinghamshire 220 in 45 overs (N. Boje 39, M.S. Kasprowicz 3-39, D.A. Cosker 2-33)
Glamorgan 224-2 in 36.5 overs (M.P. Maynard 80*, M.J. Powell 55*)
Glamorgan won by 8 wickets

28 July at Edgbaston
Glamorgan 300-8 in 45 overs (I.J. Thomas 72, M.P. Maynard 63, A. Dale 63,
  M.J. Powell 3-46)

Warwickshire 238 in 39.4 overs (I.R. Bell 86, J.O. Troughton 48, R.D.B. Croft 4-40, A.G. Wharf 3-39)
Glamorgan won by 62 runs

3 August at Sophia Gardens, Cardiff
Somerset 245-7 in 43.3 overs (K.A. Parsons 70, S.D. Thomas 2-22)
Glamorgan 118 in 22.1 overs (M.J. Powell 46, M.P.L. Bulbeck 4-39, M. Burns 3-22)
Somerset won by 107 runs (D/L Method)

4 August at Worcester
Worcestershire 202-9 in 45 overs (S. Lee 41, A. Dale 3-32)
Glamorgan 108-3 in 22.1 overs (S.P. James 41*, M.S. Mason 2-21)
Glamorgan won by 22 runs (D/L Method)

11 August at Sophia Gardens, Cardiff
Glamorgan 149-6 in 22 overs (I.J. Thomas 40, A.K.D. Gray 3-23, R.K.J. Dawson 2-31)
Yorkshire 153 in 21.2 overs (C.E.W. Silverwood 55, D.A. Cosker 4-17, R.D.B. Croft 3-27)
Glamorgan won by 21 runs (D/L Method)

14 August at Chester-le-Street (Day-night)
Durham 161 in 42.5 overs (M.A. Gough 42, S.D. Thomas 3-31, R.D.B. Croft 2-31)
Glamorgan 163-7 in 34.5 overs (S.P. James 55*, N.C. Phillips 2-38)
Glamorgan won by 3 wickets

26 August at Colwyn Bay
Nottinghamshire 226-7 in 45 overs (D.J. Bicknell 51, A. Dale 3-29)
Glamorgan 227-5 in 43 overs (I.J. Thomas 64, S.P. James 54*, N.J. Boje 2-31)
Glamorgan won by 5 wickets

2 September at Headingley
Yorkshire 167 in 44.3 overs (R.J. Blakey 47, D.S. Harrison 5-26)
Glamorgan 168-1 in 24.1 overs (R.D.B. Croft 59, I.J. Thomas 55*)
Glamorgan won by 9 wickets

3 September at Sophia Gardens, Cardiff (Day-night)
Glamorgan 280-8 in 45 overs (M.P. Maynard 87, M.J. Powell 71)

Worcestershire 177 in 36.3 overs (D.A. Leatherdale 53, D.A. Cosker 2-28,
   R.D.B. Croft 2-32)
Glamorgan won by 103 runs

15 September at Canterbury
Glamorgan 226-7 in 45 overs (M.J. Powell 74, A. Dale 43, J.C. Tredwell 3-28)
Kent 222-9 in 45 overs (M.A. Ealham 75, P.A. Nixon 49, A.P. Davies 3-37)
Glamorgan won by 4 runs

22 September at Sophia Gardens, Cardiff
Warwickshire 275-9 in 45 overs (D.P. Ostler 97, D.R. Brown 73, A. Dale 2-37)
Glamorgan 201 in 35.3 overs (M.P. Maynard 54, N.M.K. Smith 2-30, M.J. Powell 3-44)
Warwickshire won by 74 runs

14

Kasper is a Welshman

by Michael Kasprowicz

There I was standing at the top of my mark looking around the field. All I have to do is prevent the batsman scoring four runs off this last ball of the innings and Glamorgan win the Norwich Union limited-overs championship. Honestly, I felt very confident that I could land this final ball where it needed to be bowled. After all, this is what we practise time and time again in the nets. What I wasn't so sure of, however, were the two things that I had absolutely no control over. These were the ability of that particular batsman and which way the luck was to be dished out that afternoon. That, of course, turned out to be our afternoon in Canterbury.

An afternoon like that makes you realise exactly why you play this magnificent game. Sure, there is the tough pre-season spent slogging it out on the road or in the gym or the long hard days when absolutely nothing seems to go right. But believe me, in that victorious moment it is all worth every second. Whilst these are very special moments and should be shared with all the fantastic supporters, I felt it vital that the team and our support staff spend some private time together capturing this very moment in that Canterbury dressing room.

Sitting in that room, we each spoke about our own feelings in what turned out to be quite an emotional experience. Yes, there could have even been the odd tear. But for me, sitting and soaking in this special moment with my mates was the greatest part of the victory.

Another highlight had to be when some Glammy supporters started singing 'Kasper is a Welshman'. Later in the pub that night I returned the favour and taught these Glamorgan supporters a couple of Aussie songs. Come to think of it, I am pretty sure that before the end of the night I was speaking fluent Welsh!

I often get asked 'What was the difference between Glamorgan and the other counties that you have played for?' I found that I was able to identify with the massively proud identity there is to this team. This Welsh element provides an excellent bond within the team and being an Australian, I too like belting the English!

I believe that the greatest element of playing cricket professionally has to be the travel. I thoroughly enjoy the opportunity to live in another country and experience a different culture and lifestyle. To me though, the most rewarding aspect of these travels has to be the friendships and relationships formed with some fantastic people.

I feel that a special mention must be made to the coach John Derrick or was it 'Derrick John'. The League title was just reward for the all the timeless effort he puts into the team. There are also plenty of other people who all had an association with the team during the year. From Roger Skyrme, the best roomie in the business, to Len

Michael Kasprowicz bowling, watched by umpire George Sharp.

Smith and his hard-working gang, right down to the caterers and my favourite, their 'Bakewell tarts' – thanks personally from me.

Entering a new environment can always be a little daunting, but the Glamorgan boys were truly fantastic at making me feel welcome. I can safely put this down to the team warm-up. The reason being that a game of touch rugby is the preferred warm-up drill and having a background in rugby I was able to slot in rather more easily than if we had played soccer. I have no trouble going in-and-away around Crofty (not a tough move I do realise); however when it comes to soccer I have been blessed with two left feet. If soccer was the preferred choice of drill, I could have had a bit of trouble being accepted.

History and tradition are important to any cricket team. I feel very proud and privileged to be involved in such a special year and I am certainly looking forward to returning for more of the same in 2003. I see the winning of the 2002 Norwich Union One-Day Championship not as the end of a fantastic year, but more importantly the start of a long and successful era for Glamorgan cricket.

Michael Kasprowicz celebrates a wicket in the floodlit match against Worcestershire.

15

The Coach's Thoughts
by John Derrick

I think looking back over the 2002 season, if someone had said that we would win one of the one-day competitions then we would have settled for that. The win over Kent at Canterbury and the celebrations afterwards in the Bat and Ball pub will stay in my memory forever. However, 2002 was not without its disappointments, and we did not play like we should have at times in the Championship. To lose twice to Derbyshire and once to Northants and Nottinghamshire like we did, was not acceptable and this is certainly something we need to address for 2003.

But let's not dwell on the negatives as there was much to smile about and take great pride in, starting with the Cheltenham and Gloucester Trophy. We had a tricky little task first up against Lincolnshire at Sleaford, where the captain kept his head in more ways than one in order to set up an away tie with the mighty Surrey at The Oval. It turned out to be a very difficult game – not only was the captain not playing, but at the half-way mark, Surrey had scored a record 438 with Ali Brown completing an unbelievable knock.

During the lunch break between innings, I spoke to Robert Croft, our acting captain, who was very upbeat despite the mammoth score on the board. As he walked out to open the batting, he turned to the rest of the boys in the dressing room and said 'lets go out and smash it!' That's exactly what they did. Twenty off the first over, with Ian Thomas hitting Ed Giddins' first ball over deep mid-wicket for six, and the fifty came up in 3.1 overs – remarkable!

To eventually lose that game by nine runs was gutting, but I have no doubt that this match gave us great belief. Not only did it show that we

John Derrick.

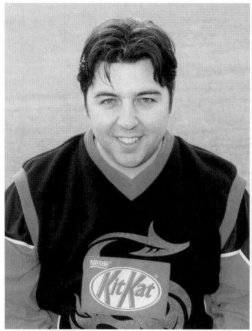

Above: Erjan Mustafa – Glamorgan's popular physiotherapist.
Right: John Derrick in his playing days with Glamorgan.

could chase anything, but there was a belief by everyone in the team that we could go on to better things. The Surrey boys could not believe what had happened either, and it was a pity that the television cameras were not there to capture our feats for posterity.

That takes us to the Norwich Union League, where some really good cricket was played throughout the season. It may be something to do with dressing up and putting on our Dragons kit, because as soon as the coloured clothing went on, we seemed to become a different side. We had our share of luck at times, but you need that in sport. I also believe you make your own good fortune, and there were a couple of potential banana skins in the games at Durham and Colwyn Bay. But we managed to successfully come through both of these games and went on to face Yorkshire, who had just won the C&G Trophy at Lord's. It was a very good time to play them, as they had had a few heavy nights after their success at Lord's. It was great to see Matthew Elliott again, and he had a meal, plus a few drinks, with the boys before the game which turned out to be a fine all-round one for young Dave Harrison, who took five wickets and then smashed a few runs to keep us in the title race.

After that, it was back home to Wales and the big game under lights at home against Worcestershire. There was some fantastic support for that day-night game at Cardiff, and the boys did really well and rose to the occasion. The batting of Matthew Maynard and Mike Powell was truly awesome and they gave us a great total to defend. The bowling was also top class and equally well supported in the field, especially from Dean

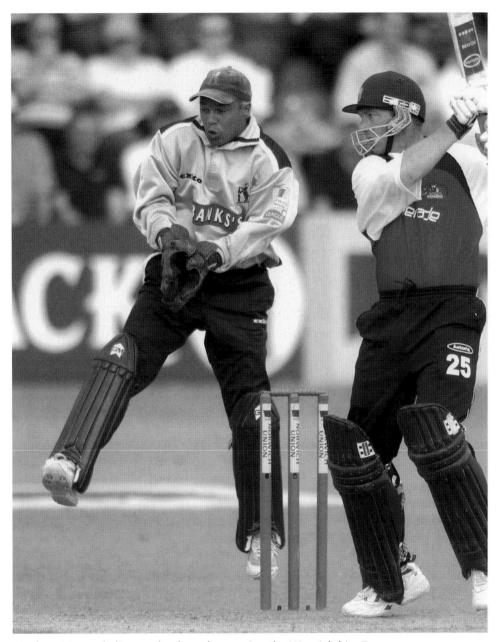

Matthew Maynard clips another boundary, against the Warwickshire Bears.

Cosker, and we came away with a fantastic result. The game was on Sky TV and it certainly showed everyone watching, whether in Wales or not, what great talent we have here in Glamorgan.

So it was off to Canterbury, and a game with Kent that would hopefully clinch the title. I must start by saying what a great attitude everyone showed the day before the

205

Cardiff 1992 – Viv Richards, Hugh Morris, Matthew Maynard, Chris Cowdry and Robert Croft during a fielding practice.

game after we arrived at Canterbury to have a net. Kent were just about to beat Lancashire when we got there, and only one net was available, plus two Astroturf wickets and a space no bigger than a netball court on which to practise. But the work that all 13 of the boys did in those two hours said it all about the attitude and desire towards winning the Norwich Union League.

The next day was the best of my cricketing career so far. I first played for the county 24 years ago in a Second XI match, so it's taken a long time, but was well worth waiting for! The precise details of the game have now become a bit of a blur, apart from Andrew Davies superbly getting Steve Waugh and those wonderful last few overs, starting with Ian Thomas taking a fine catch out at deep square leg, before Adrian Dale did his Jonty Rhodes impersonation, with the help of Mark Wallace to run out Paul Nixon. And then there was the last over by Kasper who was simply fantastic throughout the season, on and off the field. It was fitting that he should bowl the last ball to secure a fantastic win.

Boy, did we celebrate with all the supporters down in the Bat and Ball pub afterwards. It was a great result for everyone concerned and I would like to finish by thanking all the supporters at Canterbury as well as everyone else who came along at other times during the summer. The support we had all season through thick and thin was fantastic, and all of the players were very grateful for this. The players have been absolutely brilliant, and to end, I would like to thank them all for their support throughout the season, especially the captain Steve James and his vice-captain Robert Croft – thanks for a most enjoyable time.

MPM – *Our victory at Canterbury was a huge reward for all the hard work done over the past few years by John Derrick. When he had done the job before, we never really saw the best of him, as he was only in a temporary post. But John is a fine coach – he's got great technical know-how and is well respected by everyone. He's got a good rapport with the young players and has great personal qualities. He always keeps calm and placid in the dressing room, and gives off good vibes.*

SLW – *John's a good coach – he keeps things simple and puts his advice across in a straightforward way.*

ADS – *John's had to work hard for everything he's done, and he's never had things given to him on a plate. He's a lovely man to work with – I've never had a cross word with him in my time with the club, and people really seem to perform well under him. He's a very astute coach, and thoroughly deserves the success he has achieved.*

Cardiff 2002 – Steve James (with trophy), Matthew Maynard and Robert Croft celebrate winning the Norwich Union title.

Gordon Lewis, who took over as Glamorgan's First XI scorer in 2002, has known John for over fifteen years, having worked closely with him when acting as Second XI scorer, and he too is fulsome in his praise of John's approach.

GL – *Having travelled with him to numerous Second XI matches, I have found him one of the most generous and honest people I've ever known. Utterly reliable, whatever he says he will do is done. He pays close attention to detail with all matters on and off the field, and he's always got time for all of the players and people involved at every level of the club.*

John's relationship with the media is also excellent, and Edward Bevan, BBC Radio Wales' cricket correspondent, is delighted by John's fine working relationship with the press.

EB – *From the moment I first met John Derrick, when he made his Championship debut twenty years ago, he has always been courteous, helpful and friendly to the media. John had a difficult task following Duncan Fletcher as Glamorgan's coach the year after Glamorgan won the County Championship in 1997, but he has always had the support of everyone – especially the players – and he commands great respect throughout the game. He may appear easy-going, but woe betide anyone who does not give 100 per cent or does not conform to the high standards he set during his career.*

16

Testing Times at Home and Abroad

The last weekend of the 2002 season saw a large crowd at Cardiff welcome the Dragons back home for their final League game of the season against Warwickshire and the formal presentation of the Norwich Union trophy. The game proved something of an anti-climax as Warwickshire won, but there were plenty of smiles after the game as Steve James and the other members of the Dragons squad were presented with the trophy as well as commemorative medallions.

Even before the match, the players and the dressing-room staff had broad smiles on their faces, thanks to the efforts of Mark Wallace with some sticky labels. Dressing room attendant Roger Skyrme was the first person to see Wally's handiwork.

RS – *I'm one of the first people to get to the ground, just after eight o'clock. The boys usually come in about an hour later, but on this occasion, Wally was in early to create a new honours board in the dressing room. This is one of the things that Jeff Hammond brought in, and lining the walls of the dressing-room area are the names of the members of the three Championship-winning teams, the squads that won the limited-overs titles and the Glamorgan players who have appeared for England. Wally came in and on the door of the drying room, put little stickers with the names of everyone who had played in the Norwich Union games. The boys were falling around with laughter when they arrived and saw what Wally had done.*

Indeed, 2002 was not just about collective success in the one-day competition, because everyone associated with the Welsh club were proud to see Simon Jones make important strides forward in his development, and burst onto the international scene with a dramatic debut at Lord's against Sri Lanka. The twenty-three-year-old pace bowler had spent the previous winter, together with Mark Wallace, with the ECB Academy in Australia and under the tutelage of Rodney Marsh and the other coaches, Jones' talents were given a further boost.

SPJo – *Being with Rodney Marsh was tremendous. Towards the end of the stay, he said 'I cannot go on wrapping you guys up in cotton wool. It's time for you to go out into the Test arena and show what you can do.' It was a fantastic experience and when I came back I had put on over a stone in just muscle, but so much more in confidence. My father noticed it straight away, and I had so much more belief in my ability.*

Simon Jones
in action.

For several years, Simon had been on the fringe of the Glamorgan side. There was no doubting his sheer pace, but Jones, after overcoming two stress fractures, had a bit of a no-ball problem. Things had changed in 2000 when he spent some time modifying his run-up, thanks to some help from a rather unorthodox quarter – former Olympic long jumper Lynn Davies.

SPJo – *Lynn's name was first mentioned by coach John Derrick, and I was lucky enough that Gareth Davies of the Sports Council for Wales spoke to Lynn about me and explained the no-ball problem. Lynn rang me up and we then started what became weekly sessions in the nets and in the gym. I don't know what he exactly did, but within twenty minutes of our first session, Lynn spotted something and got me to change my approach.*

Then with further help from John Derrick and Jeff Hammond, Jones further modified his run-up and action in 2001.

SPJo – *I had previously run in from about 28 yards, but after three or four overs I tired. I needed to conserve energy, and with all the help of the coach's and Lynn's advice on the run-up, I found I could generate the same pace of a shorter run, and could bowl more and for longer spells. Then when I was at the Academy in Australia, Troy Coolley, the former Tasmanian pace bowler, also gave me plenty of advice and helped with my action.*

All this hard work bore fruit at the start of 2002 as Jones returned fitter and stronger after his winter in the Australian sun, and in the opening Championship game against Derbyshire, Jones claimed a career-best 6-45 with an explosive spell of pace bowling.

RDBC – *Simon had added half a yard of pace and had greater control since the previous summer and I knew all about that standing at first slip in that opening game against Derbyshire. I caught Gait in the first innings, but honestly I didn't know much about it. The ball crashed into my shoulder and somehow I managed to cling on. I think it won't be long before I'm wearing a helmet when Simon's bowling!*

In early July at Swansea, Jones produced another hostile spell of bowling in the Championship match against Essex which ended the visitors' run of five successive wins. Jones took 4 for 8 in just 16 balls to literally blow away their second innings as Glamorgan recorded an eight-wicket win.

SPJo – *It was nice to finish off the game, and help us win the match. Afterwards, Andy Flower told me that he had not faced anyone quicker than me. It was a great confidence boost for me, as Andy is one of the top-ranked batsmen in the world, and he's faced the likes of Brett Lee and Shoaib Akhtar on fast wickets.*

With the England selectors looking to add a bit of zip to their attack, Jones was selected for the First Test against Sri Lanka at Lord's. Jones made an immediate impact, although it was with his lusty batting rather than with his pace bowling. In the space of a remarkable three quarters of an hour, Jones hit 7 fours and a hugh six to the delight of a packed audience, and he left to a standing ovation after striking 44 from 43 balls. Ironically, this was six more than his father Jeff had scored in his seventeen innings in Tests for England between 1964 and 1968.

SPJo – *I found it very comforting that England batted first, because I was able to sit on the balcony at Lord's and soak in the atmosphere. I'd never played there before, so everything was new to me, but by sitting on the balcony I was able to take it all in. Before going out to bat, Nasser Hussain and Duncan Fletcher told me just to play my natural game, and not to think about blocking.*

Jeff Jones

As I walked out Craig White had a huge smile on his face. He'd seen me smash a quick 40 odd the previous year when we played at Scarborough so he knew how I'd played. I then followed my instructions and luckily things came off. The hairs on the back of my neck stood up when I eventually returned to the pavilion, and it was a fantastic feeling to get a standing ovation from all the fans, both English and Indian. It helped set the tone for the game.

Fired up by this start to his Test career, Simon then roared in as first change, and showed his talents with the ball to the packed house at Lord's.

SPJo – *I couldn't find my legs at first, and it took me a while to get use to things. Then in my fourth over, I tweaked a rib muscle, and it was a bit disappointing that I couldn't really let myself go afterwards. But it was a wonderful feeling to get my first Test wicket when Laxman edged the ball to Alec Stewart behind the stumps. Stewie then ran up and said 'Well done, Jonah. There'll be many more to come like that.' It gave me a huge lift for a Test player like Stewie to say that.*

After his fine start with bat and ball, all of the national newspapers were full of photographs of Simon and his wonderful exploits.

RDBC – *We as a County and as a country have had a breakthrough with Simon which is great, because he's playing cricket at the highest level. Kids seeing him will maybe want to be like him, or one of the other Welsh lads who has played for England. Simon's involvement will also go a long way to bringing more sponsorship and revenue into the game in Wales. He has that X-factor about him, the ability to do something out of the ordinary, and he has the potential, as long as he is left to grow and develop without being put under unnecessary pressure, to become one of the very best. If the game in Wales can benefit as a result of Simon's progress, then that is a fantastic bonus.*

Injuries after the Test prevented Simon from playing in any more Tests in 2002, as well as stifling any ambitions that Glamorgan might have harboured about gaining promotion back into Division One of the County Championship. Although he only bowled a handful of overs after his impressive debut at Lord's, there was no doubt about Simon's rich potential at Test level, and he deservedly won a place on England's Ashes tours.

SPJo – *It all seemed like a dream. My first cap at Lord's, followed by selection for my first senior tour with England. It's something every cricketer dreams of. All I had hoped for at the start of 2002 was to break into the Glamorgan side and play on a regular basis. To end the summer with my first England cap before I had been awarded my Glamorgan cap was something very special.*

But sadly, Simon's dream turned into something of a nightmare. Everything seemed to be quite promising in the early stages of the Australian series as Simon eased his way back into action after a spell on the sidelines. He delivered some hostile spells in the early games on tour, and took five wickets in the game against Western Australia at Perth.

SPJo – *The wicket in Perth was not the fastest, but it was a bit rough, and the ball started to reverse swing. That suited me down to the ground, and it was great to gradually build up speed and get back into the groove. Darren Gough was standing at mid-off, and he was a great help, with lots of advice about what I should do.*

It was nice to get selected in the attack for the opening Test of the series at Brisbane, and it was a great feeling walking out to start the game. The first session went quite well – I was told to gradually ease into things and not go bull at a gate. But with my ninth ball, I got the wicket of Justin Langer, and I was really looking forward to the post-lunch session as I was building up my pace.

But then in the afternoon session came a crunching blow as Simon tore the cruciate ligaments in his right knee as he slid to field the ball. It was something of a freak accident as his spikes got caught in the sandy sub soil as he attempted to return the ball, and it ended up with Simon leaving the field on a stretcher.

SPJo – *I knew my tour was over as soon as I did it. It was a very emotional time as I waited to go off to the hospital. The rest of the England boys in the dressing room were great to me, and Shane Warne and Andy Bichel came into the dressing room to say a few words to me. Jason Gillespie had also helped to carry me off the field on a stretcher – the Aussies may be as hard as nails on the field, but they are really genuine guys off it.*

After undergoing medical treatment in Australia, Simon returned home in late November for an operation back in the UK.

SPJo – *I've had first-class medical treatment, and after the op. it was nice to get a get well card from the Barmy Army out in Australia. It was a huge card with over a hundred signatures on it, plus a special song on the back that they had written about me. They were hoping to sing it out there, but they sadly never got a chance. It was a really nice gesture to send me the card and they are a great bunch of people.*

Naturally, I'm very upset at what has happened, but I'm determined to come back from the injury and to play again, both for Glamorgan and England. I've had stress fractures in my leg and foot before, and I've always come back after those. This time it's going to be some time before I can bowl again.

I have got to be patient – it will be a massive test for me, but I have to see it as character building. I shall be working in the gym, and I will be guided by the medical experts as to when I can bowl and when I can't. I know what is at stake. I've been told that I will play again and that's the day I'm looking forward to.

My main focus has to be my fitness and the rehab. that will be needed, but I will still stay close to the rest of the Glamorgan side, and get involved with the club. I'll go in every day, help with the youngsters, talk at the corporate boxes and do everything I can to help the team. A couple of winters ago I worked in a garage in order to make ends meet, so I know how lucky I am to be paid for doing the things I love.

Simon's upbeat mood and pride in both his own achievements for England, and those of the Glamorgan side are symptomatic of the buoyant mood in the Welsh camp. His swift progression into the national side is also evidence of the fine seam of talent emerging at the Welsh county. With Mark Wallace spending a second winter down under at the ECB Academy, and Steve Watkin at Glamorgan's own academy, passing on his wisdom and experience to the next generation of homebred cricketers, further success for the Welsh county is surely around the corner, and another chapter, yet to be written, in Glamorgan's glory days lies just ahead.

The Glamorgan team congratulate Simon Jones after he takes his sixth wicket against Derbyshire at Cardiff in 2002.

17

The Academy
by Steve Watkin

The old boots were hung up at the end of the 2001 cricket season and, after twenty years representing Glamorgan, I was thrust into the role of Glamorgan and Wales Academy director. I had a fantastic time as a player and to be given the opportunity to help groom the next generation of Glamorgan County cricketers can only be described as the next best job to being a professional cricketer.

At the time of writing, the Academy is in its second year and it will probably be a few years before its success can be judged, but I believe in its first year there was significant and faster than normal development of the players involved, which can only be good for Glamorgan and the national team.

For the record, the Academy achieves recognition and licensing from the ECB world-class performance plan and is part funded through the Coach Cymru and Elite Cymru awards from the Sports Council for Wales (SCW). The rest of the funding comes from a major contribution from Glamorgan Cricket Club. The academy director is an employee of Glamorgan Cricket Club and is also responsible for the Glamorgan Under-17 and Under-21 teams.

Basically, the objective of the Academy is to provide the selected players with the necessary knowledge required to become professional cricketers. This knowledge is not only cricket-based, but also includes lifestyle education. Of course, not all the players will go on to become first-class cricketers, but hopefully the experiences and knowledge they would have gained at the Academy will have helped them to become better and more rounded cricketers. It is hoped that they will pass on information, be it technical or tactical, to their peers raising the standard of the cricketers they come in contact with and increasing the number of talented cricketers in the region that they play.

One question is 'how does the Academy operate and what sort of things do the players do?' This is essentially my role as the academy director. The first port of call was to select the players for the Academy; this is achieved with a panel of the most respected coaches and observers in the Principality, including the academy director (i.e. myself!) the present County coach (John Derrick) and the director of the Cricket Board of Wales (Mark Frost).

The programme essentially aims to help candidates in five key areas: technical, tactical, physical, psychological and a programme of lifestyle modules. The facilitators of each component were chosen for their expertise in their fields. Each player is assigned a technical coach who they work with on a one-to-one basis up to twice a week. There are also specialist sessions that work on specific areas, for example the playing of short, fast deliveries. The Academy uses the likes of Matthew Maynard,

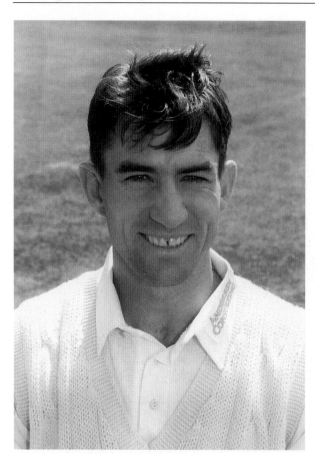

Steve Watkin.

Robert Croft, Steve James and Tony Cottey – present county cricketers who have a wealth of knowledge and experience, which passed on to the next generation in a structured environment can only be good for the game.

Glamorgan has always prided itself on the number of home-grown players who have come through the Cricket Board of Wales (CBW) or Welsh schools' structure; the Academy can only help this process. The 1990s and the early millennium are testament to this sound structure that is now in place and the success of the last decade has a lot to do with the excellent team spirit and pride representing, in effect, the national Welsh side. Jacques Kallis aside, the victorious Wales team that played England in 2002 was made up of products of the Welsh structure – and with the likes of Bangladesh having Test status, perhaps a Wales international team isn't too far away. A lot of credit must go to the likes of Tom Cartwright (former national coach), Peter Walker (former director of the Cricket Board of Wales) and Mark Frost – as well all the coaches who gave up their spare time to coach the regional, national and club junior sections. These are the people responsible for the system that is now in place and allow me the opportunity to pick from a pool of talented cricketers.

We may not produce any more players than we do at present, but the intention is that the able cricketer should be ready – both technically and physically – at an earlier

Mark Frost (right) at the launch of a coaching initiative in the new Indoor School at Cardiff.

Jonathan Hughes – a rising Glamorgan star, and one of the next generation of attacking batsmen.

age than they would be otherwise. The result of this will be a greater number of talented cricketers to select from, which would create keen competition for places and a higher standard of cricket in the long term.

At present, there are about fourteen county academies all hoping to produce the next Test cricketers. I only hope that we give the system time to take effect and don't rush into changes before the academy system has been given a fair chance. The main benefactors will be the England cricket team and who knows, in the not too distant future, we may be back challenging the outstanding Australians for world supremacy. After all, if we don't start competing, the present academy director may well be looking for a new job! If success does come at national or club level, it will be satisfying to know that the structure and set up in Wales will have helped the team called England – or perhaps it is time to rename the team Great Britain or the British Lions, one can only dream!

18

Glamorgan – The Future
by Steve James

So what does the future hold for Glamorgan? Arguably the last ten years have been the most successful in the club's history, but is the club in good enough shape to sustain this success?

I believe that it is. I believe that the players involved in these successful years have established a 'Glamorgan way' of doing things, which is being passed down to the younger players, and that this progressive learning process will continue in the future.

Firstly, there is the manner in which the side conducts itself on the field. In 2001, the MCC established its Spirit of Cricket award – to be voted upon by the first-class umpires and to be presented to the county side that in their opinion has best upheld the spirit of the game during the season. Glamorgan won that vote – unanimously apparently – in both 2001 and 2002. And if I am honest, I cannot envisage another county taking our title from us in the near future.

Next, there is the dressing-room spirit, which is regarded as the strongest and most fervent on the county circuit and which obviously stems from Glamorgan's unique identity of representing a country. There is humour and banter, as well as sensitivity to other people's needs and requirements. There is even a team song, initiated by Australian Matthew Elliott and the evocative words written by Owen Parkin. At the moment, Darren Thomas has the honour of leading that song after every victory. This is indeed an honour and in time he will bravely pass it on to another proud Dragon.

Then there is the work ethic, which has improved year by year. It is now quite incredible and Glamorgan is generally regarded as the fittest county side. And it is not just on the fitness side, technical practice is also assiduously attended to. The building of the new indoor centre at Cardiff has helped enormously here. No longer are rushed trips to Neath necessary when unexpected rain has washed out nets at HQ. Glamorgan now has a ground with accompanying facilities of which it can be truly proud.

However, no one should fool themselves that it has all been a bed of roses during this decade. For it has not. There have been many dark days, as there always will be in any sport, especially in cricket where the slings and arrows of fortune seem to be at their most extreme.

The greatest difficulty for any successful side is how to maintain that success as that side dissipates. That will be the biggest challenge facing Glamorgan in the next few years but I am confident that it can be overcome. The likes of Matthew Maynard, Robert Croft, Adrian Dale and I will all have to be replaced at one stage or another. Glamorgan has always prided themselves on the production of its own players and that is to be applauded. It is a source of much pride that there are no so-called EU-qualified players

Steve James celebrates with a happy Dean Cosker at Taunton in 1997.

on the staff, at a time when their presence is causing uproar as well as threatening to undermine the whole ethos of county cricket. The recently formed academy under the astute eye of Steve Watkin will, I'm sure, continue the good work of the old Welsh Schools system, which must take credit for producing the majority of the successful side of the 1990s.

There are, however, times when astute signings have to be made from outside. Alan Butcher, Colin Metson, Roland Lefebvre and Alex Wharf instantiate this. Sadly, there are many others who do not. When Hugh Morris retired in 1997, it was felt that the gap could be bridged from within but unfortunately, time has proved that not to be the case. But hindsight is a wonderful tool. Only the overseas opening batsmen, Matthew Elliott and Jimmy Maher have proved capable of any real consistency.

I think that Dan Cherry will prove to be a good long-term bet as a successful county opener. He seems to possess the requisite attitude and application, as well as an aptitude for batting long periods of time. His appearance and mannerisms bear an uncanny resemblance to Hugh, so let us hope that he assaults the Glamorgan record books in the same way. Ian Thomas has shown tremendous attitude too, albeit of an altogether more aggressive nature. He is not fazed by anyone or anything. I think his future may well lie in the middle order. Jonathan Hughes is another who has demonstrated enormous talent, possessing a wide array of shots and an alluring sense of having the time to play those shots.

Dan Cherry.

The advent of the ECB Academy has advanced the progress of two of our young players Mark Wallace and Simon Jones, so much so that Simon has already been capped by England. My guess would be that Mark will be the next Welshman to achieve that honour, although the steadily improving batsman Mike Powell, like Mark reared in Abergavenny, might have something to say about that.

The introduction of the central contract system will have a profound effect on Glamorgan's future, as it will on all the other counties. Indeed, Simon will probably not appear much for Glamorgan in the near future if he continues his remarkable progress. This should not produce any feeling of bitterness or regret in Wales, for I feel that it is one of the prime responsibilities of every county to produce players capable of playing international cricket. Let us continue to do so.

David Harrison proved at the back end of 2002 what a fine prospect he is, coming into the one-day side during the tense run in for the National League title, and performing nervelessly. His tall action will always ensure that his bounce troubles the best batsmen and I believe that he has it in him to become a genuine all-

David Harrison.

rounder. Duncan Fletcher first noticed this potential in 1999 and he is a pretty shrewd judge of talent, as his perspicacious picks of Marcus Trescothick and Michael Vaughan for England have proved. Watch out too for David's younger brother, Adam, who is showing every sign of being as good as, and maybe even better than, his brother.

Whatever, the future looks bright. I am aiming to be part of it for as long as my aching body permits, but when that does eventually give in, I will be the most avid of followers and watchers. For there is something very special about playing for Glamorgan, and may that always be the case.

And finally, a word from Chris Cowdrey, who enjoyed a brief career with Glamorgan in the early 1990s after a highly successful career with Kent from 1977 until 1991. He captained Kent between 1985 and 1990, but he readily admits that some of his happiest playing days were with the Welsh county.

Chris Cowdrey

I experienced one of the most enjoyable seasons of my cricket career playing for Glamorgan in 1992. Any success the club has had comes as no surprise to me, due to the wonderful spirit amongst Glamorgan players and supporters alike. But please can you stop coming down to Canterbury to collect your trophies!